Keen Kutter Planes
The Simmons Hardware Company

Alvin Sellens

4880 Lower Valley Road, Atglen, PA 19310 USA

Published by Schiffer Publishing Ltd.
4880 Lower Valley Road
Atglen, PA 19310
Phone: (610) 593-1777; Fax: (610) 593-2002
E-mail: Schifferbk@aol.com
Please visit our web site catalog at **www.schifferbooks.com**
We are always looking for people to write books on new and related subjects. If you have an idea
for a book please contact us at the above address.

This book may be purchased from the publisher.
Include $3.95 for shipping.
Please try your bookstore first.
You may write for a free catalog.

In Europe, Schiffer books are distributed by
Bushwood Books
6 Marksbury Ave.
Kew Gardens
Surrey TW9 4JF England
Phone: 44 (0) 20 8392-8585; Fax: 44 (0) 20 8392-9876
E-mail: Bushwd@aol.com
Free postage in the U.K., Europe; air mail at cost.

Designed by Joseph M. Riggio Jr.
Type set in Korinna BT

ISBN: 0-7643-1610-9
Printed in China

Contents

Background

The Simmons Hardware Company was a leader in the wholesale hardware field throughout its years of existence. Many articles and vignettes have been written about the company and its founder E. C. Simmons. A number of these writings, including some of those sponsored by the company, contain conflicting information. An attempt has been made to correlate and combine all available information into a brief history using the source considered to be the most reliable.

The portions of this book devoted to woodworking planes contain information extracted from Simmons Hardware Company catalogs and modified in some instances by review of actual hardware. Many of the illustrations herein were drawn from catalogs. The quality of each illustration is a function of the quality of the source catalog. In many cases, Simmons catalogs were printed using extra-thin stock and stock that has yellowed severely with age. The catalog data is accurate in general but often misleading in detail. It is noted that several of the catalog illustrations are not correct with reference to positioning of the number designations. It is suspected that the illustrations are early artist renderings that were never updated to agree with the actual hardware. Discrepancies are pointed out in the text in some cases.

Woodworking planes were standard tools of every carpenter, joiner, and cabinet maker long before the Simmons Hardware Company was founded. In the 1860s several hundred craftsmen were making and selling wooden planes bearing their own marks and a few companies were getting into mass production. Adjustable woodworking planes became available in quantity in 1870 when Stanley Rule and Level Company offered a full line of metal and wood bottom bench planes. Other makes of planes were available in the 1870s and 1880s but were not as widely advertised as Stanley.

Early Simmons Hardware Company catalogs offered a full line of wooden planes made by Ohio Tool Company of Columbus, Ohio. At that time Ohio Tool was one of the largest makers of wooden planes in the United States. The line included bench, moulding, and a variety of special purpose planes. The early catalogs also offered an extensive line of Stanley metal and wood bottom planes. In addition, various early Simmons catalogs listed Davis, L. Bailey, Chaplin, Siegley, and B planes. The separate bench plane irons (cutters) listed in the early Simmons catalogs were Butcher and American. The maker of the American cutters was not stated.

Keen Kutter plane cutters were offered in the Simmons Hardware Company general catalogs starting in 1891. Planes bearing the Keen Kutter mark were first offered in 1895.

Foreword

This volume contains a history of Simmons Hardware Company and associated information prepared from the viewpoint of a tool collector. Also included is the information available on woodworking planes, routers, scrapers, and spoke shaves offered by Simmons Hardware Company under their brand names Keen Kutter, Simmons, Chip-A-Way, Oak Leaf, Bay State, and Bailey's Blued. Inasmuch as complete plane collections are not available for review, this report is somewhat less than definitive. It should, however, provide a sound basis for definition as additional information becomes available.

This book assumes that an item offered in one catalog was available until the next catalog was issued. General catalogs were not printed for each year and at one point in time were published at three and four year intervals. In a few cases interim catalogs and brochures have been noted and have been taken into consideration

Simmons Hardware Company: A Brief History

The Early Years

The story of the early years of Simmons Hardware Company of St. Louis, Missouri, and the events preceding it is essentially a chronology of the life of its founder, E. C. Simmons. Considered by some of his contemporaries to be the greatest salesman of his time, Edward Campbell Simmons built and presided over Simmons Hardware Company, which became the largest wholesale hardware firm in the country. Although Simmons was in complete control of all phases of the business, his greatest interests and talent were in salesmanship and selling. He pioneered the use of traveling salesmen for jobbing firms and at one time the company employed more than six hundred people on the road. Extensive use of advertising, detailed catalogs, and personal contact with the customer were characteristics of Mr. Simmons and of the Simmons Hardware Company. Simmons knew each of the company salesmen personally and kept in contact with each one through meetings and letters. The employees familiarly referred to him as No. 8 because his initial as written resembled the number.

E. C. Simmons was born September 21, 1839, in Frederick, Maryland, the son of Zachariah T. and Louisa H. Simmons. He moved to St. Louis, Missouri, with his parents at the age of six. The part of the journey through the mountains was made by stagecoach, there being no railroads through the mountains at that time. The balance of the trip west was made by steamboat. They arrived in St. Louis on February 26, 1846. Zachariah listed his occupation in St. Louis at various times as a city weigher, a collector, and as a merchant.

After grammar school and a little high school, E. C. Simmons obtained a job at Child, Pratt and Company, a wholesale hardware firm in St. Louis. He was sixteen years old at the time. His salary for the first year was $150.00. Duties of his first job consisted of removing goods from the shelves, dusting and replacing the goods. In a short time he was promoted to errand and stock boy. Later he was afforded the great privilege of carrying the store key and opening the store each morning. He was soon greeting early customers and became a salesman by virtue of being the only one on the premises first thing in the morning. Simmons was queried at the age of seventeen as to his ambition in life. He answered, "To have the most satisfactory hardware store in the world."

After working at Child, Pratt and Company for about three years, Simmons obtained a job on January 1, 1859, as a clerk at Wilson, Levering and Waters, another wholesale hardware company in St. Louis. Simmons was a nephew of Mr. Levering, one of the owners of the firm. The firm later became Levering, Waters and Company. Simmons was admitted to the firm as a junior partner on January 1, 1863. Eighteen months later Mr. Levering died and the firm name was changed to Waters, Simmons and Company.

When Waters retired on January 1, 1871, Simmons bought his interest in the firm and renamed it E. C. Simmons and Company. I. W. Morton became a partner in the business at that time, having purchased a one fourth interest. Shortly after acquiring controlling interest, Simmons expressed a desire to restructure the business in order to allow other employees to participate in future growth. A charter was granted December 15, 1873, to incorporate the firm on January 1, 1874, under the name Simmons Hardware Company. Several people criticized the move as merely a means of limiting liability and avoiding payment of debts. Simmons and Morton weathered the criticism and proceeded to incorporate. It has been reported that Simmons Hardware Company was the first mercantile firm to be incorporated in the United States. The new corporation was capitalized at $200,000. Simmons and Morton were the primary stockholders and several other employees purchased smaller numbers of shares. Initial investors included H. M. Meier, R. H. Stockton, J. E. Pilcher, E. H. Sublett, C. D.

E. C. Simmons.
From the 1910 Simmons Hardware Co. catalog

Smiley, and A. E. Dann. Originally the company had a rule that only employees could own stock but the rule was quickly broken when a shareholder quit and refused to sell his shares. E. C. Simmons was named president of the new firm and I. W. Morton became secretary and treasurer. W. H. Waters, one of the previous owners, was named vice president even though he did not own any stock.

In 1859, Wilson, Levering, Waters and Company was doing business at 51 North Main in St. Louis. Prior to the incorporation, the business had moved to 220-224 North Main. There were several wholesale hardware houses in St. Louis at that time and they were all clustered within a few blocks of each other. Retail merchants would come to the city once a year and order merchandise as needed for the entire following year. They could walk from one wholesale house to another to select the desired merchandise at the most attractive price. There were not any complete catalogs at that time and very few traveling salesmen.

The new company moved into a new building at the northeast corner of Main Street and Washington Avenue shortly after the corporate charter became valid. The building was leased for five years. Their 1877 letterhead listed their address as 601, 603, and 605 North Main. The new corporation had forty-one employees including thirteen salesmen. Morton became vice president in 1877 as well as treasurer, and R. W. Stockton was elected secretary. During the first few years of operation the business was operated essentially as a proprietorship. There were no board meeting minutes and no reports. None of the officers knew how a corporation was supposed to function.

The early years of Simmons Hardware Company included considerable innovation and expansion. Simmons described themselves on an 1874 flyer as Importers and Manufacturer's Agents. An 1877 letterhead says Importers and Jobbers. The Keen Kutter trademark had already been established for axes and was being rapidly expanded to include other edge tools. Simmons led the way in the 1870s in stocking a wide variety of sporting goods along with standard hardware. They advertised guns, rifles, and pistols, both American and imported. Pocket cutlery from Wosterholm, Rodgers, and Walden was listed in 1877.

Cutlery was a specialty of Simmons Hardware Company throughout its life. As a boy, E. C. Simmons was fascinated with pocket knives and this interest led him to ask for employment in a firm that handled knives. Later, cutlery was emphasized because it was a high profit line and because it was easy to store and ship. The salesmen were encouraged to carry large sample cases of cutlery and to show it first and last to each merchant visited. Each salesman was expected to have ten percent of his sales in cutlery. One advertisement boasted that the Keen Kutter mark was put on more than one million knives per year. Another catalog stated "We regularly carry 3000 to 4000 different styles of pocket knives alone."

When the building lease ran out in 1879, Simmons Hardware had again outgrown its quarters. It was moved to a new building at Ninth Street and Washington Avenue at that time.

The 1860 St. Louis City Directory listed the address of E. C. Simmons and his parents as 118 Olive Street. He later moved to 1814 Olive Street. Mr. Simmons said that he preferred to live downtown close to the business. He married Carrie Welch in 1866 and their son, Wallace D., was born in November of the following year. Two other sons, Edward H. and George W., were born later. The family moved to 2721 Olive Street in 1877. Simmons was active in public life and often entertained company salesmen in his home. One letter mentioned entertaining forty salesmen in his home at one time.

All three of the Simmons boys had worked at menial jobs in the company during school vacations. After completing college, Wallace D. Simmons the oldest son, worked in various departments in the company to gain overall familiarization with the hardware business. He was named as a director of the company and assistant treasurer on March 8, 1892.

In the early years I. W. Morton was in charge of all buying and Simmons's specialty was selling. As the size of the business increased, department managers and a general manager were appointed to reduce the day-to-day duties of the officers. Simmons and Morton continued to exercise general oversight of their particular areas.

Simmons Hardware Company was a growing and well-organized business in the latter part of the nineteenth century and had become the leading hardware jobbing firm in the country. Sales were exceeding one million dollars per month at that time. E. C. Simmons and I. W. Morton resigned from their positions as president and vice president respectively January 3, 1898, and turned the business over to new management.

The Old Guard

The phenomenal success of Simmons Hardware Company was at least partially the result of the expertise and dedication of a few top men in the organization. E. C. Simmons had the ability to select and retain top quality managers. He made a practice of promoting from within the company and rewarding talent by both recognition and remuneration. As one means of recognition, names of various company officers and top employees were used on special brand merchandise. Certain of the company branch warehouses were also named after notable employees and officers. Almost all of the company officers and department heads had been salesmen at one time or another. That experience assured that they knew hardware and were familiar with the needs of the customer. In later years Simmons referred to these top managers as *The Old Reliables*.

Isaac W. Morton was vice president of Simmons Hardware Company for many years until he stepped down from active management in 1898. He was a partner in E. C. Simmons and Company and a major stockholder in Simmons Hardware Company. Morton was in charge of all buying for the company which complemented Simmons's expertise in sales. After stepping down from active management he remained active in company operation and top management as an advisor. The Morton-Simmons branch warehouse in Wichita, Kansas was named in his honor. Morton was employed as a bank teller prior to his association with E. C. Simmons and Company in 1871.

Isaac W. Morton.
From *Forty Years of Hardware*

9

J. E. Pilcher was second vice president of the company at one time and was appointed first vice president when I. W. Morton resigned the position. Pilcher was in charge of the large cutlery department which was a specialty of Simmons Hardware. Several items bearing his name were advertised prominently in early catalogs. J. E. Pilcher's Farrier's Pincers and J. E. Pilcher's Cant-B-Beat Hand Saw were among those items listed.

H. M. Meier started to work for Waters, Simmons and Company at the age of fifteen and rose to the office of vice president of Simmons Hardware Company in charge of all salesmen. Various early catalogs featured his name on items such as H. M. Meier's Coal Pick, H. M. Meier's Polar Ice Saw, and H. M. Meier's Lead Pencils.

Saunders Norvell worked for Simmons for thirty years starting at the age of seventeen as a store clerk. He worked his way up through the company as salesman, sales manager, and finally as a vice president. S. Norvell's Shovels and S. Norvell's Chip-A-Way Axes were offered in early catalogs. Norvell resigned from Simmons Hardware Company in 1901 and took over control and management of Shapleigh Hardware Company, which became a major competitor of Simmons.

R. H. Stockton was an original investor when the Simmons Hardware Company was incorporated. He was secretary of the firm at one time and later became a vice president. He served the company at various times as salesman, sales manager, and as head of the cutlery department. Several catalog items bear his name: examples are R. H. Stockton's Scythe, R. H. Stockton's Gold Dust Axe, and R. H. Stockton's Chip-A-Way Axe.

A. E. Dann was hired by E. C. Simmons and Company in 1871 as a stock clerk and rose to the position of company treasurer. He was an original investor in Simmons Hardware Company.

William Enders was a super salesman from the Texas area and later became vice president. His name appears on a wide variety of merchandise sold by the Simmons Hardware Company. The names Wm Enders Oak Leaf and Enders Oak Leaf were used on an entire line of tools, safety razors, padlocks, and other items. Some items were listed as Wm Enders Manufacturing Company.

Other men who were prominent in the company and whose names were used on advertising, letterheads, invoices and catalogs include Henry Beneke, Tom Dymond, H. M. Finch, A. Latham, C. D. Smiley, and E. H. Sublett.

New Management

E. C. Simmons retired from day-to-day management of Simmons Hardware Company in 1898 but continued in the position of Chairman of the Board of Directors. He and I. W. Morton resigned as president and vice president respectively but retained offices at the company headquarters as an Advisory Committee. Wallace D. Simmons, the oldest son of E. C. Simmons, was appointed company president. He had been active in company management for several years prior to the retirement of his father. Edward H. Simmons, the second son, was appointed to the board of directors and made assistant secretary of the corporation. George W. Simmons, the third son of E. C. Simmons, became vice president a few years later.

The new management team assumed control and detail operation of the company and management duties were eventually divided among the three sons. Wallace D. Simmons was responsible for overall company policy and direction. Edward H. was in charge of sales and advertising and George W. took over as head of purchasing.

During the first few years of the new management, the company continued to expand. A letter dated 1904 stated that Simmons employed 1600 people plus 280 salesmen. It also stated that the company served 45,000 customers. There is little doubt that Simmons Hardware Company was the largest and most aggressive hardware jobber in the country at that point. Keen Kutter cutlery was given the highest possible award at the St. Louis Exposition of 1904 and Keen Kutter and Walden pocket knives were given a similar award at the 1905

W. D. Simmons.
From the 1912 Simmons Hardware Co. catalog

Exposition in Portland, Oregon. It was also during this period that the branch warehouses were established.

Around the turn of the century Simmons deviated from their status as wholesale-only and opened retail stores in St. Louis and Chicago. The retail stores were intended to be used to establish prices, test new products, and to try different forms of advertising. The Chicago store was operated under a separate name and was not widely known as a company business. Operation of the St. Louis store drew criticism from some of the local merchants who accused Simmons of unfair competition. The store in St. Louis was closed in 1905 and the one in Chicago was sold at about the same time.

Continued expansion of the company or even maintaining its position was hampered by several factors during the early years of the twentieth century. The proliferation and growth of mail order houses threatened the existence of retail hardware stores as well as the hardware jobbers. Simmons Hardware Company boasted that they refused to sell to the mail order houses and urged other jobbers to do likewise. They also urged the retail dealers to refuse to carry or push standard brands carried by the mail order houses. Local and regional wholesale firms were taking an increasing share of the available sales volume. Personnel problems were also dampening factors. The young management team had been educated in eastern schools and brought in eastern friends to fill responsible positions. Naturally, the older employees resented this outside interference with their duties and areas of influence. The resentment was at least a contributing factor to retirement of some of the valuable members of the old guard including H. M. Meier and J. E. Pilcher. Saunders Norvell resigned as vice president and took over management of Shapleigh Hardware Company. The loss of an experienced sales manager was compounded in that Norvell took along several top men in the organization including W. H. Yantis head of the sporting goods department. Loss of the services of these individuals to an aggressive competitor was a severe blow to the Simmons Hardware Company.

E. C. Simmons resigned as director May 6, 1906, but remained as chairman of the board. This ended the advisory committee inasmuch as I. W. Morton had died in late 1903.

Simmons Hardware Company initiated a massive advertising campaign early in the 1900s to help counter the mounting competition. The advertising was largely aimed at increasing the name recognition of their largest special brand, Keen Kutter. This advertising blitz was a primary factor in allowing Simmons to maintain its dominant position in the hardware jobber field.

The First World War caused a shrinkage of volume due to the shortage of consumer goods, and the brief business downturn following the war was a continuing drag on profits. Shortly after World War I, Winchester Repeating Arms Company formulated their grand plan to manufacture a wide range of sporting goods, cutlery, and hardware and to sell these goods directly to retail hardware stores. Needless to say, the hardware jobbers including Simmons Hardware Company were violently opposed to the idea inasmuch as the jobbers would be bypassed completely. The scheme involved signing one hardware store in each town into an agency agreement with Winchester, which would give them the exclusive right to sell the new line of Winchester products and to buy directly from Winchester. Each hardware store was to buy a quantity of Winchester stock and pay a monthly fee for the privilege of being a Winchester Store. E. C. Simmons was very vocal in his opposition to the Winchester Plan and cautioned the retail dealers not to participate in the scheme. In a personal letter dated 12/27/19, he stated " —and yet I know enough to fully believe that every Retail Hardware Merchant who goes into this deal now will regret it, and scarcely any of them will prosper under the arrangement". George W. Simmons also voiced his opposition to the Winchester Plan in a February 1927, convention speech. He stated at that time that Simmons was dropping Winchester guns from their next catalog.

The death of E. C. Simmons on April 18, 1920, resulted in more management problems for Simmons Hardware Company and the Simmons brothers were apparently about ready to quit the hardware business. In April 1922 George Simmons approached Winchester Repeating Arms Company with a proposal to sell the Simmons Hardware Company stock belonging to he and his two brothers. This amounted to controlling interest in the firm. George apparently had the backing of his brother Edward and made the initial negotiations without the knowledge of his brother Wallace D. who was then president of the company.

Negotiations progressed rapidly and on June 26, 1922, the sale was completed and the Simmons family no longer owned Simmons Hardware Company. The sale price for the Simmons family interest in the firm was about 3.4 million dollars plus some stock in the new companies that proved to be of questionable value.

The Winchester Years

Upon the purchase of Simmons in 1922, Winchester Repeating Arms Company immediately set about merging the Winchester and Simmons holdings. A holding company was established and named Winchester-Simmons Company. This company consisted of Winchester on one side and eleven Associated Winchester-Simmons Companies on the other. The Simmons Brothers were replaced by new management from the Winchester firm. The Associated Winchester-Simmons Companies were essentially the old Simmons distribution facility in St. Louis plus ten branch warehouses. These companies were assigned to take over all selling of the new Winchester product line and the Winchester side of the holding company was to do all manufacturing. Accordingly, the manufacturing interests of the old Simmons Hardware Company were transferred to the Winchester side of the holding company and Simmons took over four Winchester distribution warehouses.

The Simmons employees were demoralized by the abrupt sale of the company. The salesmen were in a difficult position when attempting to answer questions in the field. The retail dealers had been told repeatedly by Simmons management that the Winchester Plan was a bad deal and suddenly Simmons was part of the plan. Some of the retail dealers no longer trusted the Simmons firm and took their business elsewhere and several of the older salesmen quit in disgust. The sales management and the buying departments of Simmons were moved to Winchester headquarters in New Haven, Connecticut, which further disrupted the business routine of the company.

Simmons salesmen had the exclusive right to sell the new line of Winchester merchandise to the Winchester Stores. However, other jobbers could also sell their own line to these stores. The Winchester line was difficult to sell in many cases because prices were not always competitive with Keen Kutter and other brands. Start-up costs and inexperience kept Winchester manufacturing costs high. Prices were generally above those of the competition even though the Winchester side was often selling at a loss.

The Winchester people who were selling the agency plan to the retail dealers did an excellent job. There were ultimately more than 6400 Winchester Stores, which was approximately one-fourth of all retail hardware stores in the country. These outlets provided a broad base for sales of the new Winchester merchandise. The store operators were pledged to push Winchester products where possible and all advertising was aimed in that direction. However, the Winchester product line was slow in building up and the confidence of the dealers eroded. It was part of the Winchester plan to offer only high quality merchandise. Quality and name brand recognition were to be the main selling points. In general, the quality pledge was kept but often at the expense of competitive pricing. The percentage of Winchester products sold through the stores never reached expected levels even after the product line was complete. The Winchester management suspected that the old Simmons people were pushing Keen Kutter at the expense of Winchester. The old-line Simmons people complained that all the promotion and sales effort favored Winchester. Actually, the primary factor in the lagging Winchester sales was probably price.

The Winchester side of the company was reorganized February 5, 1929, after suffering severe losses on most of the new products. The reorganized company declined to take over the agency agreements in effect with the Winchester Stores. The exclusive right of the Simmons companies to sell the Winchester line was also terminated and Winchester started to sell name brand merchandise on the open market. At that time the Winchester-Simmons Companies reverted to their old status as Simmons Hardware Company. The grand Winchester Plan had been given a fair trial and had failed. The predictions of E. C. Simmons regarding the plan were proven to be accurate. Simmons hardware Company had failed to profit under the arrangement and the Winchester stock bought by the dealer agents had never paid a dividend.

The Final Years

The years following the Winchester era could be characterized as a struggle for survival. The branch warehouses were all closed and all manufacturing activity was terminated with the exception of paint products. The 1930 catalog included several Winchester items that were probably the residue of the merchandise in stock when the Winchester Plan collapsed.

The depression starting in late 1929 made it difficult to mount a recovery program. The company went into bankruptcy in 1934 and was reorganized the following year. In their best year Simmons Hardware Company distributed forty million dollars worth of merchandise but sales had eroded. The 1935 and 1939 catalogs showed that the company emphasis had shifted from tools to housewares. The cutlery section had even been reduced, except that pocket knives were still a specialty.

The assets of the Simmons Hardware Company were sold to Shapleigh Hardware Company on July 1, 1940. The selling price was approximately 2.75 million dollars in cash. The reign of what was once the largest hardware jobber in the country had come to an end.

The Shapleigh Era

All of the assets of Simmons Hardware Company including the trademarks were bought by Shapleigh and the holdings of the two companies were immediately integrated. Keen Kutter and several other Simmons house brands were continued after the sale. Shapleigh headquarters was moved to the buildings previously occupied by Simmons. The catalogs were quickly revised to include specialty items of both companies. Keen Kutter and Shapleigh Diamond Edge items were often listed on the same page. The Keen Kutter logo was retained unchanged for several years but was ultimately changed to include the word Shapleigh's in lieu of E. C. Simmons.

Shapleigh made a valiant effort to recover after the lean years of World War II but the days of the big hardware jobbers were numbered. In January, 1959, the employees were told that the company would be liquidated. The remaining stock was sold and the doors of the Shapleigh Hardware Company were finally closed for business in late 1959.

Catalogs

E. C. Simmons wrote regarding the catalog of 1899, "It is, I am sure, to the hardware dealer the most valuable book ever published." The 1899 is indeed a masterpiece among catalogs. It has 1992 pages describing literally thousands of items and includes 9759 illustrations. The high quality paper used in this catalog is just as readable today as it was one hundred years ago.

INTERESTING STATISTICS.

THIS CATALOGUE

Contains (including Index) Exclusive of Inserts   -   4200 Pages

Contains (Exclusive of Inserts)   -   21,535 Illustrations

Contains (Exclusive of Inserts)   -   -   79,137 Items

Edition   -   -   -   -   25,000 Copies

Edition (25,000 Copies) Weighs ($\frac{1}{2}$ Million Pounds)   250 Tons

Paper Used   -   -   -   -   16 Car Loads

Tar Board used in Binding, 750 Bdls. 50 lbs. each,

     37,500 lbs.,   -   -   -   - $18\frac{3}{4}$ Tons

Cloth Used in Binding, 6500 yds. Art Canvas, 1 yd.

     Wide   -   -   -   -   58,500 Square Feet

All Pages put End to End would reach over 8600 Miles, or one-third of the way around the World.

Ink Used   -   -   -   -   2500 lbs. or $1\frac{1}{4}$ Tons

Statistics from the 1908 Simmons Hardware Company catalog

The Simmons Hardware Company published one of the world's first completely illustrated hardware catalogs in 1880. Each item in that large volume was illustrated and described. The catalog was assembled by I. W. Morton in his spare time and took eighteen
months to compile. It is said that he worked nights and weekends to complete it on sched-
ule. Simmons stated later that this 1880 catalog was the most important single item that
contributed to the success of the company. Several of these catalogs still exist. It is noted
that there were very few Keen Kutter items listed at that time. Keen Kutter axes were featured
and placed in a prominent position in the book. The first catalog was an immediate success
and additional general catalogs were published at three and four year intervals. One copy
was provided free to each dealer; additional copies were available at one point for fifteen
dollars each. A later catalog stated that additional copies were not available at any price.
The 1908 catalog, sometimes referred to as The Encyclopedia of Hardware, contains 4200
pages and 79,137 items. Twenty-five thousand copies of this huge catalog were printed.
Starting in 1912, the catalog illustrations were reduced in size and lighter paper was used.
Fifty thousand copies of the 1912 catalog were printed. Content of the catalogs were also
reduced at that time and greater emphasis was placed on small specialty catalogs. A January 1912 Simmons letter offered to send their new catalog along with the first order if the
order would make up a 100 lb. shipment.

Large general catalogs were published as follows:

    1880 No letter designation
    1883 No letter designation
    1887 No letter designation
    1891 No letter designation
    1895 No letter designation
    1899 No letter designation. One abridged, two full versions and six supplements
        were printed.
    1904 Catalog F (copyright 1903)
    1908 Catalog G. Some are coded GG
    1912 Catalog H
    1913 Catalog K
    1914 Catalog L
    1915 Catalog M
    1917 Catalog N
    1918 Catalog P
    1921/22 Catalog R
    1924 Catalog S, Winchester-Simmons. There are ten different catalogs of this
        date. One for each warehouse
    1927 Catalog T, Winchester-Simmons
    1930 Catalog U
    1935 Catalog V. An abridged version is coded V1
    1939 Catalog Z
    1940 Loose-leaf catalog. Shapleigh issued update pages in late 1940 but did not
        replace the cover until 1942

Specialty catalogs were published by Simmons Hardware Company starting in 1877.
Dozens of these smaller catalogs were printed and provided free to the retail stores upon
request. The large general catalogs made frequent reference to these specialty books and
recommended that the dealers obtain them. Some of the specialty catalogs are shown in
the catalog table. Correlation of catalog numbers with the dates shown should be helpful in
dating other Simmons Hardware Company paper items. It should be noted that the same
series of numbers used for specialty catalogs was also used for brochures and other paper
items.

Specialty Catalogs

Catalog	Date	Product
No. 331	1899/00	Lamps
No. 341		Cutlery
No. 348	1900	
No. 350		Mill Supplies
No. 363		Padlocks
No. 371		Sewing Machines
No. 401	1901/02	Lamps
No. 411	1902	Bicycle Sundries
No. 427	1902/03	
No. 434	1903	Baby Carriages
No. 436	1903	Laclede Bicycles
No. 442	1903/04	Sporting Goods
No. 443	1903	Builders Hardware
No. 462	1904	
No. 487	1905	Tool Book
No. 519	1906/07	Lamps
No. 538N	1907	Sporting Goods
No. 565	1907/08	Builders Hardware
No. 719	1909	Laclede Bicycles
No. 788	1909/10	Lamps
No. 1367	1912	Bicycles and Sundries
No. 1819	1915	
No. 1941	1916	Aluminum Ware
No. 2247	1917	Harness

Advertising

World's Fair Exhibit advertising fan

Extensive advertising was a hallmark of the Simmons Hardware Company throughout most of its life. Topping the list of advertising was the wide use of illustrated catalogs discussed above. Massive exhibits at the World's Fairs and Hardware Conventions were also features of the company policy. Many of the World's Fair give-away items of the early 1900s are still in existence and command premium prices from collectors. Hand fans, postcards, and brochures are examples of these advertising handouts. The huge Simmons exhibit at the 1904 Exposition in St. Louis was awarded the grand prize. The exhibit was made up of 12,407 Simmons name brand tools including more than 5,000 axes.

A blitz of magazine advertising was launched in the early part of the twentieth century. Full page ads in such publications as the *Saturday Evening Post* were used to tout the Keen Kutter name at the national level. Fifty-four different publications with a combined circulation of sixteen million carried Keen Kutter advertising during this period. The company also did some local advertising in newspapers and on billboards in areas where sales were poor.

Keen Kutter Airplane.
From *The Great American Hardware Story*

Another unique form of advertising was the Keen Kutter airplane bought in 1919. The airplane attracted a lot of attention at hardware conventions and similar gatherings inasmuch as airplanes were still a novelty at that time. Free rides were given to dealers and clerks. The national advertising campaign even included a Service Bulletin published during World War I.

Salesmen, retail merchants, and long time employees were often awarded various trinkets such as axe head pins in appreciation of exceptional service. These awards were intended to motivate the recipients and were mobile advertisements for the Simmons special brand line.

The slogan "A jobbers First Duty is to Help His Customers to Prosper" was more than mere words to the Simmons Hardware Company. The company went to great lengths to support the retail dealers with advertising aids while at the same time enhancing name recognition of a special brand. Electrotypes were provided without charge to encourage local advertising. Signs for use in stores, in street cars, and on fences were available free or at nominal cost. Complete store window displays and displays for special occasions were available to all dealers. Animated window displays were available on short-term loan to good customers. The Simmons salesmen were cautioned against loading up the dealers with slow moving merchandise and excessive stock. The dealers were constantly encouraged to use mail orders to keep their stock small and current. During lean years, Simmons provided extra credit to allow good customers to buy in anticipation of later sales.

The retail stores were encouraged to use Keen Kutter letterheads, invoices, paper bags and even wrapping paper. Store fixtures such as showcases, display stands, and paper holders were listed in the catalogs and could be purchased on the same terms as retail merchandise.

Manufacturing

Simmons Hardware Company was basically a distributor of everything normally sold by a retail hardware store. Their primary business was buying in large quantities from many manufacturing companies and selling in smaller quantities to retail merchants. However, they also dabbled heavily in manufacturing at various times. An early reference to manufacturing is noted in the 1880 catalog. A Cucumber wooden cistern pump is shown in that catalog as being manufactured by Simmons Hardware Company St. Louis, Missouri. In the 1904 catalog Simmons described themselves as Manufacturers and Distributors.

In 1922, Simmons owned controlling interest in three manufacturing firms:
- Walden Knife Company, Walden, New York
- Mound City Paint and Color Company, St. Louis, Missouri
- Roanoke Spoke and Handle Company, Roanoke, Virginia

At the time of the Simmons acquisition by Winchester, control and management of these manufacturing companies were immediately moved to the Winchester side of the holding company.

Simmons owned and operated the St. Louis Saddlery Company for many years and manufactured a wide line of horse-related goods including several types of harness and collars. The 1904 catalog states under the horse goods section, "Our modern factory, equipped with the latest machinery enables us to produce the best of everything at a low price". The factory was still listed in the 1921 catalog but subsequently disappeared from the listings along with most of the saddlery products.

The Grant Leather Corporation of Tennessee was bought by Simmons in mid-1919 with the intent of consolidating its operation with the St. Louis leather goods factory. A new building was erected in Kingsport, Tennessee to house the operation. However, before the new building had been completed, the market for leather goods decreased dramatically. Apparently, the new factory never opened for business. James Carroll, in his book *Fifty Stepping Stones*, lamented that this factory was a great mistake.

Simmons began buying pocket knives from the Walden Knife Company of Walden, New York, about 1874 and bought controlling interest in the firm in 1902. At that time there was a move afoot to consolidate the major knife manufacturers into a single combine. Simmons bought Walden to protect their supply of knives and to avoid getting involved with the combine. Additional capital was provided to expand the Walden facilities and Simmons eventually consumed all of the factory output. Prizes were awarded to Simmons and Walden at the 1905 Exposition for the superior excellence of quality and finish of their pocket knives. The 1908 catalog has an impressive illustration of the Walden Knife Company "Where we make all of our Keen Kutter pocket knives". It states that the factory occupies 60,000 square feet and employees 535 skilled workmen. A later reference states that the Walden facility occupies over 100,000 square feet and that 700 skilled workmen are employed. A 1910 letter stated that the factory in Walden was making 500 dozen pocket knives per day. A portion of the assets of Walden was transferred to the Winchester facility in New Haven, Connecticut, in September 1923 and the knife company was dissolved.

The Roanoke Spoke and Handle Company of Roanoke, Virginia was chartered March 20, 1916. This factory manufactured spokes, tool handles, baseball bats and similar articles. The factory building was destroyed by fire in 1925 and never rebuilt.

Simmons operated a paint factory at Main Street and Clark Avenue in St. Louis starting in 1915. They bought the Mound City Paint and Color Company September 30, 1920 and combined the two operations to manufacture a full line of paint products. There was also a branch factory in Philadelphia, Pennsylvania. The factory in Philadelphia was shut down and its assets transferred to New Haven when Winchester took over the manufacturing facilities. The main factory of the paint firm in St. Louis was operated by Winchester for several years without much success. The capital stock was transferred back to Simmons Hardware Company in 1927.

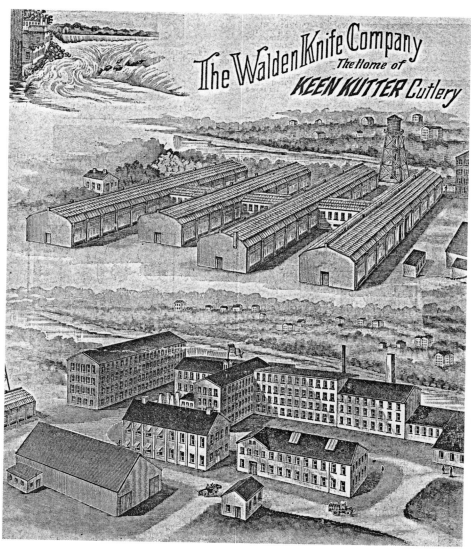

The Walden Knife Company, the Largest Factory of its Kind in the World.
From the 1918 Simmons Hardware Company Catalog

The Wardlow Cutlery Company was founded in March 1909 and the name was changed to Wm Enders Manufacturing Company in 1911. The company was established to avoid putting the Simmons name on certain imported cutlery. This company owned the trademark rights for Wm Enders Oak Leaf and leased the rights to Simmons Hardware Company for one hundred dollars per year. At one time Simmons distributed an extensive line of Oak Leaf tools and hardware. The Wm Enders Manufacturing Company did not have any employees and did not conduct any business. The company address in New York was merely a letter drop.

The Howard Cutlery Company was another non-active concern established to facilitate importing of certain merchandise from England. The firm did not do any actual business.

The Enders Sales Company, sometimes listed as Enders Razor Company, was established January 26, 1911. The purpose of this company was to separate the Enders safety razor business from the Simmons and Oak Leaf names so that the razors could be sold to other jobbers. Some jobbers were reluctant to buy direct from Simmons Hardware Company. Shipping to other jobbers was made direct from the supplier and billing was done through Simmons. The Enders Sales Company was a paper-only concern and did not do any business.

Simmons established the Stanwood Motor Car Company in October 1919. It was the intent of this company to develop and build an automobile for marketing through hardware dealers. Several cars were built but there proved to be very little demand and the project was abandoned. Simmons also financed the Almetal Manufacturing Company in 1915 to manufacture a home washing machine. Almetal home laundry machines having integral water heaters were offered in the 1918 Simmons catalog.

The Manufacturers Distributing Company was chartered in January of 1916 for the purpose of financing certain special articles requiring additional development prior to manufacture. This company did not do any actual manufacturing.

The catalogs issued after the breakup of the Winchester-Simmons combination in 1929 did not mention Simmons as being a manufacturer except for paint products. It is assumed that the company retreated from manufacturing at that time.

Warehouses

Prior to 1902 Simmons operated from a central location in St. Louis, Missouri. Salesmen covered the entire United States and even Cuba, but with a few exceptions, all goods were shipped from St. Louis. Direct factory shipments were occasionally arranged for carlots of heavy or bulky merchandise. Shortly after the turn of the century Simmons began to experience increasing competition from regional and local wholesalers that were beginning to open at every rail junction. The local jobbers could provide next day delivery to many retailers whereas Simmons had to ship and trans-ship from St. Louis. To meet this competition in one area, Simmons purchased a warehouse in Ogden, Utah in 1902. The warehouse was used to store staple goods, especially heavy items. Orders from the surrounding areas were billed from the main office in St. Louis but shipped from Ogden. This warehouse was closed in 1908 but served as a prototype for future branch warehouses.

During the September 1904 board meeting the president of the company spoke of the desirability of opening branch warehouses in various parts of the country in order to retain their existing share of the wholesale business. Accordingly, a holding company was organized to acquire warehouse facilities in several cities.

The 1907 catalog listed the following warehouses:
Simmons Hardware Company, St. Louis, MO
Hurty-Simmons Hardware Company, Minneapolis, MN
Dymond-Simmons Hardware Company, Sioux City, IA
Standart-Simmons Hardware Company Toledo, OH
Morton-Simmons Hardware Company, Wichita, KS
Simmons Hardware Company, New York, NY
Simmons Hardware Company, Ogden, Utah

Some of the branch warehouses were named for executives of the company or the manager of that particular branch. For example, Tom Dymond was an exceptional salesman and later became a vice president and manager of the Dymond-Simmons Hardware Company. W. H. Standart was also a vice president of the company. I. W. Morton was a long time associate of E. C. Simmons and a major stockholder in the company.

The Morton-Simmons Hardware Company Building.
From the 1908 Simmons Hardware Company Catalog

The Hockaday Hardware Company of Wichita, Kansas, a wholesale hardware firm, was purchased by Simmons to form the Morton-Simmons Hardware Company in 1906. A new building was erected to house the operation.

Each of the warehouses carried a complete stock for their respective area and each had a separate catalog. The catalogs were identical in most cases except for the covers and the title pages. A 1910 catalog stated that the combined space occupied by the main facility and all of the warehouses was more than 1.5 million square feet or 35 1/4 acres.

The Associated Simmons Hardware Companies was set up in 1911 as a trust to control and manage the various warehouses and the manufacturing companies owned and controlled by Simmons. Each of the warehouses became a separate subsidiary company serving a specific part of the country. Each had their own salesmen, credit departments and billing departments.

A new warehouse company was chartered January 3, 1912, in Philadelphia, Pennsylvania. A Boston, Massachusetts, facility was formed in 1916 by acquisition of the Frye-Phipps Company, an old wholesale firm of that city. A New Jersey corporation operated warehouses in Memphis, Tennessee, and Los Angles, California, for short periods starting in 1921.

At the time of the Simmons acquisition by Winchester in 1922, the Simmons warehouse companies were officially renamed Winchester-Simmons. However, the new names were never applied to the detail workings of at least some of the companies. Inasmuch as the Winchester-Simmons organizations were to handle sales of the new line of Winchester products, they took over the existing Winchester distribution facilities in Chicago, San Francisco, Kansas City and Atlanta. New companies were formed in some locations. In other cases the Winchester facilities were closed within a short time and the stock absorbed by the Simmons warehouses in the affected areas. Ten Winchester-Simmons Distribution Companies were chartered. Some of the companies had facilities in more than one city.

The 1924 Winchester-Simmons catalog listed warehouses as follows:

St. Louis, MO
Atlanta, GA
Chicago, IL
Kansas City, MO
Los Angles, CA
Minneapolis, MN
Philadelphia, PA
Portland, OR
San Francisco, CA
Sioux City, IA
Springfield, MA
Toledo, OH
Wichita, KS

Ten of the distribution points listed above were still in operation in 1927. The breakup of the Winchester-Simmons combination in early 1929 apparently signaled the demise of the branch warehouse operations. Only the St. Louis and Philadelphia facilities were in operation at the end of 1929. The Philadelphia warehouse was still operating in 1932 but the 1935 catalog listed only the St. Louis facility.

The Morton-Simmons Hardware Company of Wichita, Kansas was closed in 1929 and the building was sold the same year to another hardware jobber. The building, known as the Keen Kutter Building, still stands. Its attractive design with its distinctive tower is a credit to the city and to the area. A faded Keen Kutter logo painted more than ninety years ago is still visible. The building has been renovated and was opened as a hotel in 1999.

Trade Marks and Special Brands

Simmons Hardware Company was basically a wholesaler or jobber as they were some-times called. They stocked merchandise under brand names of both major and minor manu-facturing companies and at the same time contracted with numerous manufacturers to obtain goods marked with Simmons special brand names. More than 700 of these special brand names were used by Simmons at various points in time.

Keen Kutter

The best known special brand in the hardware field during the first half of the twentieth century was *Simmons Keen Kutter.* E. C. Simmons coined the name in 1865 or 1866 for use on an axe made to his specification. The 1880 catalog states that over 7000 dozen Keen Kutter axes were sold in 1878 and that the demand has increased every year since their introduction in 1866. Another Simmons catalog states that Keen Kutter was chosen in 1870 as a logo for the company. Still another catalog states that the first Keen Kutter tools were made in 1869.

All of the above dates are possibly correct. It is probable that Keen Kutter axes were manufactured and sold starting in 1866 and that Keen Kutter was adopted in 1870 as a general name for top quality edge tools. Several of the trademark applications submitted by Simmons in 1906 state that the mark has been used continuously by the company since 1868. Store signs were available 1910 proclaiming that Keen Kutter tools and cutlery had been offered for forty years. All of these bits of information indicate that 1870 was the actual starting point of the general Keen Kutter line.

The account of how the Keen Kutter name started has been told and retold many times and has been garbled on occasion. Saunders Norvell, a close associate of E. C. Simmons, tells the story succinctly in his book *Forty Years of Hardware.* His account is quoted:

> "I have heard E. C. Simmons tell the story on several occasions. He said that in the early days the Lippincott axe was very popular. It was a thinner axe in the blade and for this reason cut better in soft woods. The Simmons house sold a lot of these axes, but they found the manufacturer would sell any good retail buyer at about the same price as to them. The head of this axe factory called and Mr. Simmons sought some protection. None was forthcoming, so that night Mr. Simmons went home angry and disturbed. He said he retired early but woke up in the night and thought about axes. Finally he got up, hunted up a block of wood and with his penknife whittled out a long slim axe — even slimmer than the Lippincott. When it was finished to his satisfaction, without any premeditation, he wrote in pencil on the fresh pine wooden axe: Keen Kutter. The next day he started out to find a manufacturer who would make his new axe, and succeeded. Thus was started the Keen Kutter trademark which in time became the leading jobbers special brand in the country. So again it is illustrated how great oaks from little acorns grow, If Mr. Simmons' rest that night had not been disturbed, we might never have had the problem of special brands in the hardware trade."

Simmons had sufficient confidence in his new pattern of axe that he immediately or-dered two thousand dozen from Isaiah Blood of Bollston, New York. These were quickly sold and the brand name for axes was firmly established. The words Keen Kutter were used initially on one variety of axe but usage was slowly expanded to other types of merchandise. In the 1880 catalog, the mark was applied to cutting tools only; axes, hatchets, saws, scythes, adzes, bill hooks, shears, scissors, files, stones, razors and knives. Usage was gradually expanded until by 1895 a wide variety of cutting tools were available with the Keen Kutter name. Throughout this period the Keen Kutter brand name was applied to cutting tools only with the minor exception that trowels and punches were offered. By the early 1900s the Keen Kutter name could be found on almost any tool or gadget a hardware store was apt to stock. George Simmons noted in a 1920 address that the company had a line of Keen Kutter items consisting of 2170 patterns and 4000 sizes. E. C. Simmons once stated that he considered the trademark to be worth in excess of $100,000.

Mr. Simmons insisted that only first quality merchandise be sold under the Keen Kutter name. All Keen Kutter items were highly advertised as having a full replacement guarantee against defects. One reference boasted that 100,000 Keen Kutter drawing knives had been sold and not one returned as defective.

A list of items known to have the Keen Kutter name or logo is shown in Appendix A.

Keen Kutter Marks - Prior to 1905

An 1877 Simmons Hardware Company Letterhead

An 1877 letterhead is the earliest noted indication that Simmons claimed Keen Kutter as a trademark. See illustration.

It is curious that none of the early catalogs indicated that Keen Kutter was a trademark name. The 1895 catalog was the first to carry that notation. Each axe page of that catalog carried the statement *Trademark Keen Kutter Registered*; however, the pocket knife and razor pages were not so annotated. It is probable that Simmons initially registered the mark for axes only under the 1881 trademark law. The early trademark law was often misunderstood and generally ignored. It wasn't until early 1905 that the United States passed a comprehensive trademark law that was widely accepted and enforceable.

Numerous ways of presenting the words Keen Kutter were used prior to 1905 for specific types of merchandise. The marks were often changed from one catalog to the next. The words were written in a variety of forms including block letters, script and in several fanciful patterns. However, there is no indication that any particular design or style was claimed as a trademark.

Keen Kutter Shield mark

The earliest documented form of what might be called a Keen Kutter logo is a shield design with the general appearance as shown in the illustration. The shield was not standardized and therefore appeared in several variations. Usually the shield outline included the words E. C. Simmons and quite often the word Celebrated was added. Just what was celebrated is not clear. This general type of shield logo was used from 1880 thru 1904 on axes, hatchets and other handled cutting tools. It was also used on numerous paper items such as invoices and postcards and on give-away items. The mark phased out starting in 1905 and was not shown in the 1908 catalog.

Keen Kutter Marks - 1905 and Later

The familiar Wedge & Bar logo was adopted by Simmons in early 1905. There was, of course, an overlap of marks until existing stock was sold. Some early 1905 invoices and letterheads carried both the shield and the new wedge and bar. Starting in 1906, Simmons registered the wedge and bar trademark with and without the words Keen Kutter inside of the mark. They also registered the words Keen Kutter without a border. At least twenty-five separate registrations were granted for various types of merchandise and markings. Typical trademark applications and grants are shown in Appendix B. Several of the 1906 registrations stated that the mark had been used continuously by the company for fifteen years. It is true that the words Keen Kutter had been used for many years prior to that time; however, the wedge and bar had definitely not been used in the trade literature prior to 1905. It can only be assumed that Simmons fudged the facts somewhat in the trademark applications to implement rapid approval. As a matter of interest, Simmons referred to the logo as "— the words Keen Kutter and a figure of wedge shape having three-sided projections at its sides and on which said words appear".

Wedge and Bar logo, 1905 - 1911

Wedge and Bar logo, 1912 - 1946

The illustrations top and right show the wedge and bar logo as it appeared in Simmons Hardware Company catalogs and other advertising literature starting in 1905. The words St. Louis U.S.A. were changed to Cutlery and Tools in 1912. The later mark was used for many years and was continued for some time even after Simmons was sold to Shapleigh Hardware Company in 1940. The last noted example of this particular mark is on a 1946 invoice.

Information about Shapleigh Hardware Company for the 1940s period is sparse. It is known that sometime between 1945 and 1951, the wedge and bar logo was changed to include the word Shapleigh's as shown in the illustration. Many of the original trademark registrations were renewed by Shapleigh after 1940 and were renewed again by Val Test Distributors, Inc. after the liquidation of Shapleigh.

Additional examples of Keen Kutter marks are shown in Appendix C.

Wedge and Bar logo. 1947 - 1959

Simmons

Many hardware and paper items were marked Simmons, E. C. Simmons, S. H. Co., and with various S. H. Co. symbols. When Keen Kutter items of the same type were offered, Simmons items were second quality to the KK merchandise. The Simmons marks were also applied to many items not having a Keen Kutter counterpart. In many cases the Simmons name or symbol was used in conjunction with another special brand name such as Simmons Keen Kutter or Simmons Run Easy.

SIMMONS

S. H. CO.'S*.

Examples of Simmons marks

Various types of these marks were used throughout the life of the company. Some examples are shown below.

True Blue

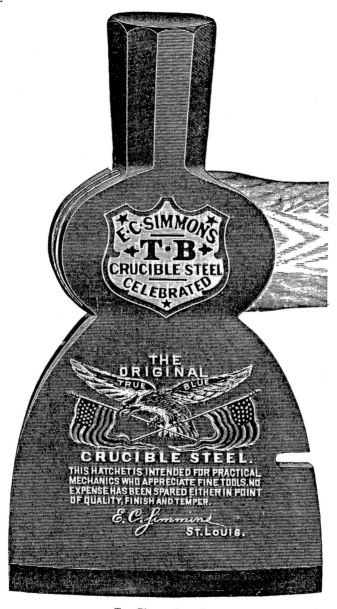

True Blue trademark

True Blue tools were offered from 1891 thru 1903. The name was listed in the 1899 catalog as a registered trademark. The True Blue tools were second quality to similar Keen Kutter items.

Blue Brand

Blue Brand tools were offered from 1904 thru 1906. The name was listed in the 1904 catalog as a registered trademark. The Blue Brand tools were second quality to similar Keen Kutter items.

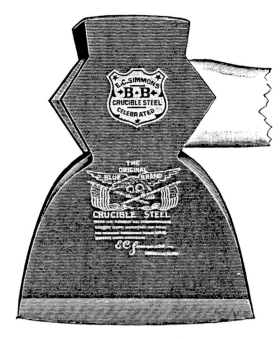

Blue Brand trademark

Chip-A-Way

Simmons Hardware used the trademark name Chip-A-Way on cutlery and tools around the start of the 20th century and was granted at least four registrations of the mark for various classes of hardware. The mark was first noted in the 1891 general catalog where it was used on an R. H. Stockton Chip-A-Way axe. Stockton was a Simmons employee at that time.

CHIP-A-WAY

Chip-A-Way trademark 1895

In 1895 an S. Norvell's Chip-A-Way axe was listed and the Chip-A-Way name was applied to chisels and drawing knives. The mark was enclosed within a scalloped border in some cases. The name was listed as a registered trademark starting in the 1895 catalog.

Chip-A-Way trademark 1908

A wide variety of hardware bearing the Chip-A-Way mark was offered in 1904 and 1908. It was used as a second quality brand at that time. Included were wooden planes, pocket knives, hammers and axes. Starting in 1908, the mark was generally enclosed within a double line. See illustration. The 1908 Simmons catalog states that there are 300 patterns of Chip-A-Way pocket knives available and that they are American made. There was a Chip-A-Way Cutlery Co. in England at some point; however, the relationship with Simmons, if any, is not known.

The Chip-A-Way name had almost disappeared from the catalogs by 1914. Only a few items such as files remained and these were probably left over from previous years.

Oak Leaf

Simmons offered Oak Leaf brand tools and other items for more than forty years. However, most of the Oak Leaf items extant were sold during the 1912-1930 time period. The Oak Leaf is one of the many Simmons special brands despite an apparent effort to disguise the fact in some cases. A chronology of usage is provided to aid in understanding the evolution of the mark and to aid in dating individual items.

Oak Leaf logo, 1895

The Oak Leaf name first appeared in the Simmons catalog of 1891. This catalog lists a handsaw marked H. M. Meier Oak Leaf with a design of an oak leaf branch with an acorn. The 1895 catalog shows the same handsaw plus several H. M. Meier Oak Leaf hatchets. See 1895 illustration. The 1904 and 1908 logo is similar to that shown for the hatchet except that the leaf does not have an acorn. Both of these catalogs state that Oak Leaf is a registered trademark. Henry M. Meier was vice president of Simmons Hardware Company in 1896 and at one point he was in charge of all the salesmen.

Oak Leaf logo, 1904-1908

The 1903 and 1908 catalogs provided a positive indication that Oak Leaf was a Simmons brand. See illustration. These catalogs also include some tools bearing a simple Oak Leaf logo without the Meier or S. H. Co. name. Apparently the Meier tools were being phased out at that time. It should be noted that all Oak Leaf logos used thru 1908 showed a branch with more than one leaf.

Oak Leaf Logo, 1912

Starting in 1912 the Oak Leaf logo was changed to a single leaf with the words Oak Leaf inside the leaf border. In some cases the words Wm Enders and St. Louis U.S.A. were also included in the design. This logo was used on many types of tools and on several other items including padlocks. In 1918 the mark was changed to read Walden, N.Y. rather than St. Louis. The Walden mark was retained through 1924.

The 1930 catalog still had many Oak Leaf items but the number was reduced from previous catalogs. It appeared that the Oak Leaf was being closed out. The mark at that time had been changed back to read St. Louis in lieu of Walden. By 1935 the Oak Leaf items had been completely eliminated except for padlocks which were still offered in 1939.

Williams Enders was a salesman for Simmons Hardware Company in 1887 and later became sales manager and vice president of the company. He was also president of the Wm Enders Manufacturing Company.

Three trademark applications were filed in 1919 by the Wm Enders Manufacturing Co. of Walden, New York requesting registrations of the Oak Leaf mark. The mark was leased to Simmons Hardware Company and all Oak Leaf brand merchandise was controlled and distributed by Simmons. The Wm Enders Manufacturing Company was a paper-only concern.

Bay State

Tools bearing the name Bay State were listed in Simmons Hardware Company catalogs starting in 1884. From 1914 thru 1934 Simmons used the Bay State name on a wide variety of second and third quality hand tools. The name was applied to an entire line of axes, hatchets, hammers, cement tools, augers, chisels, tool chests, etc. and was even used for a work bench. There was also a Bay State padlock. The catalog illustration indicate that most of the Bay State tools offered during this period were marked with paper labels. This temporary type marking probably accounts for the relative scarcity of items marked Bay State.

The illustration shows two items marked with the Bay State name. It is probable that these tools are of Simmons origin in the 1914-1934 time span.

There was a Bay State Tool Company at one time and several other firms used Bay State as a special brand name for items other than tools.

Additional Brands

Numerous other special brand names were used by the Simmons Hardware Company. In some cases the name was used for many years and other names appeared in only one catalog. In a few cases a Simmons special brand name has been noted that did not

Bay State mark

appear in any general catalog. Apparently these items were short term sales merchandise offered only by the salesmen or in sales catalogs. Not all of the special brand names were registered trademarks.

Some of the brand names were used in conjunction with Simmons, E. C. Simmons, S. H. Co. or an S. H. Co. symbol. In several cases a special brand name was listed in various Simmons catalogs with and without the Simmons name applied. Several of the names were used in multiple combinations such as Black Jack, Keen Kutter Black Jack, and S. H. Co. Black Jack.

A list of the special brand names known to have been used by Simmons Hardware Company is shown in Appendix D.

Company Motto

THE MOTTO

"The Recollection of QUALITY Remains Long After the PRICE is Forgotten."

Trade Mark Reg. in U. S. Patent Office. —*E. C. SIMMONS*

Simmons Hardware Company motto

"The Recollection of QUALITY Remains Long After the Price is Forgotten" was the motto of the Simmons Hardware Company. The preface of the 1899 catalog, written by E. C. Simmons, states that this has been my motto for life. In this preface, retail merchants were exhorted to always emphasize quality rather than price in their selection of stock. Quality was a prime advertising point throughout the life of the company. The motto never appeared on any actual hardware but was used ad-infinitum on catalog pages, media advertising, cartons, store fixtures, wrapping paper, give-away items, invoices and almost anywhere else that the customer might look. The motto, coined by E. C. Simmons, was first stated as a question, "Is not quality remembered long after price is forgotten?" but was later changed by Simmons to the form of a statement.

The motto was originated in 1898 and was used in a company pamphlet about that time. It was used extensively in the 1904 catalog and continuously thereafter until the Shapleigh Hardware Company ceased operations. The motto was registered as a trademark in October 1905. The trademark application stated that it had been in continuous use since 1903.

A 1907 catalog mentioned "a motto originated many years ago by Mr. E. C. Simmons, the founder of the business, *Our first duty is to help our customers to prosper*". The motto or saying was modified later to *A Jobbers first duty is to help his customers to prosper.* Later catalogs referred to this saying as a maxim or an expression rather than a motto.

Keen Kutter Wooden Planes

The Simmons Hardware Company offered Keen Kutter wooden bench planes from 1895 thru 1929. Standard sizes of smooth, jack, fore, and jointer planes were included. These planes were of top quality and all had front knobs.

Wooden Planes - Saw-Tooth Logo

Keen Kutter wooden bench planes were first offered in the 1895 catalog. Smooth planes, with and without handles, were available along with jack, fore, and jointer planes. These are the family of flat bottom planes used for general purpose smoothing and fitting and for reducing stock size.

Catalog pictures show the words Keen Kutter written on the side of each plane. However, the early planes extant do not have any name or logo on the side. The logo was incised on the toe end as well as on the cutters. All planes are made of beechwood and have front knobs. The knobs on the earliest listings were coated with thick black paint and said to be Ebonized. The bodies of these planes are approximately 2 1/4 inches deep; which is slightly less than wooden planes made by most makers of the era. All of the planes were fitted with tapered Keen Kutter double irons that had been sharpened and hand whetted on an oilstone. These planes appear to be identical in construction to the top quality wooden planes offered in the Ohio Tool Company catalogs. There is little doubt that Ohio Tool made the planes for Simmons.

Neither the planes nor the cutters were designated with a K number as commonly used for later Keen Kutter tools.

The plane illustrations in the catalogs do not show which Keen Kutter logo was used on the cutters or the planes. The separate replacement cutters shown in the 1891 thru mid 1899 catalogs were shown with rectangular saw-tooth mark as shown in the illustration.

Rectangular Saw-Tooth mark

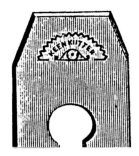

Semi-Circular Saw-Tooth mark

Cutters shown from mid 1899 thru 1905 have a semi-circular saw-tooth mark. See illustration.

Many planes having the semi-circular mark have been noted in collections and shops. These same observations have failed to reveal a single plane or plane cutter having the rectangular mark. It is therefore considered doubtful that such a logo on planes actually exists. As a matter of interest, the rectangular logo has been noted on chisels.

The following planes were listed:

Wooden Smooth Plane

Wooden Smooth Plane $40 - $65
    Offered: 1895 thru 1905
    Material: Beechwood
    Length: Not specified 1895-1903, 8 inches 1904-1905
    Width of Cutter: 2, 2 1/8, 2 1/4 inches
    Type of Cutter: Double
    Front Knob: Ebonized 1895 thru mid 1899, Lignum Vitae mid 1899 thru
        1903, Applewood 1904 thru 1905

Logo: Semi-Circular Saw-Tooth. Located on the toe end and on the cutter
These were general purpose smoothing planes used to prepare the surface
of a workpiece. They were short to allow usage on a small surface. The
throat was normally narrow and the cutter was set for a fine shaving

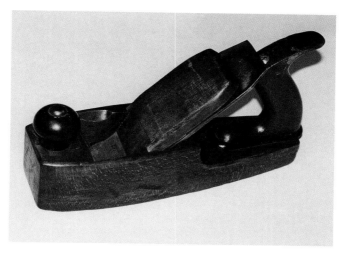

Wooden Smooth Plane, handled

Wooden Smooth Plane, Handled $50 - $75
    Offered: 1895 thru 1905
    Material: Beechwood
    Length: Not specified 1895-1903, 10 1/2 inches 1904-1905, 9 1/2 inches
        observed
    Width of Cutter: 2, 2 1/8, 2 1/4 inches
    Type of Cutter: Double
    Front Knob: Ebonized 1895 thru mid 1899, Lignum Vitae mid 1899 thru
        1903, Applewood 1904 thru 1905
    Logo: Semi-Circular Saw-Tooth. Located on the toe end and on the cut-
        ter
    These were general purpose smoothing planes used to prepare the sur-
    face of a workpiece. The handled variety was easier to use especially for
    long periods. They were short to allow usage on an small surface. The
    throat was normally narrow and the cutter was set for a fine shaving

Wooden Jack Plane

Wooden Jack Plane $35 - $60
    Offered: 1895 thru 1905
    Material: Beechwood
    Length: Not specified 1895-1903, 15 inches 1904-1905
    Width of Cutter: 2, 2 1/8, 2 1/4 inches
    Type of Cutter: Double
    Front Knob: Ebonized 1895 thru mid 1899,Lignum Vitae mid 1899 thru
        1903, Applewood 1904 thru 1905
    Logo: Semi-Circular Saw-Tooth. Located on the toe end and on the cutter
The jack plane is the workhorse of the plane family. It is a convenient
middle size and is used for any and all bench plane functions. This size is
one of the most common of Keen Kutter planes
The illustration shows one jack plane with an applewood front knob and a
similar one with an ebonized knob

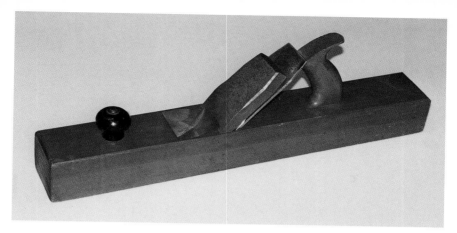

Wooden Fore Plane

Wooden Fore Plane $45 - $75
  Offered: 1895 thru 1905
  Material: Beechwood
  Length: Not specified 1895-1903, 20 inches 1904-1905
  Width of Cutter: 2 3/8, 2 1/2 inches
  Type of Cutter: Double
  Front Knob: Ebonized 1895 thru mid 1899, Lignum Vitae mid 1899 thru
    1903, Applewood 1904 thru 1905
  Logo: Semi-Circular Saw-Tooth. Located on the toe end and on the cut-
    ter
The fore plane is actually a short jointer. It is sometimes used before the
jointer plane allowing the jointer to be kept extra sharp to make the final
cut for edge joining

Wooden Jointer Plane

Wooden Jointer Plane $60 - $85
  Offered: 1895 thru 1905
  Material: Beechwood
  Length: 26, 28, 30 inches

Width of Cutter: 2 1/2, 2 5/8 inches each length
Type of Cutter: Double
Front Knob: Ebonized 1895 thru mid 1899, Lignum Vitae mid 1899 thru 1903, Applewood 1904 thru 1905
Logo: Semi-Circular Saw-Tooth. Located on the toe end and on the cutter

The jointer is the longest of the bench plane family. It is used where maximum accuracy is desired. Its extra length and weight reduces waviness to a minimum

Boy's Smooth Plane

Banner logo

Wooden Planes - Banner Logo $45 - $65

A boys' wooden smooth plane 5 1/2 inches long and several standard sized bench planes bearing the banner logo, see illustration, have been noted. They were all marked on the toe end and on the double cutter. These planes are made of beechwood including the front knob. Both ends of the boys smooth plane are coated with an orange paint that appears to be original.

This variety of plane is not listed in any of the general catalogs. It is probable that they were shown in an interim or sale catalog or perhaps they were included as part of a youth's tool chest outfit. The banner logo was used on other types of tools, primarily chisels, in the 1895 thru 1905 time span. It is assumed that the planes bearing this logo are of the same period.

Wooden Planes - Wedge & Bar Logo

A line of Keen Kutter bench planes bearing the familiar wedge & bar logo was offered starting in 1906. Smooth planes with and without handles, jack, fore, jointer, and razee type planes were available. These are the family of flat bottom planes used for general purpose smoothing and fitting and for reducing stock size.

The planes are made of beechwood and have front knobs. The knobs on the earliest listings were coated with thick black paint and said to be Ebonized. Later planes have smaller knobs made of walnut. The bodies of the planes are approximately 2 1/4 inches deep; which is slightly less than wooden planes made by most makers of the era. All of the planes were fitted with tapered Keen Kutter double cutters which had been sharpened and hand whetted on an oilstone.

Catalog illustrations show the logo on the side of each plane. These pictures are somewhat misleading. Early jack, fore, and jointer planes (1906 thru 1917) have the logo incised on the upper surface forward of the front knob. The logo is on the left side of early smooth planes. The later variety (1918 and later) of all sizes have the logo incised on the toe end.

Wedge & Bar logo, wooden planes

Most planes of this vintage are marked with the wedge & bar logo having St. Louis U.S.A. inside of the logo outline. However, wooden planes made after 1917 do not have the St. Louis wording. See illustrations.

The early variety of these planes was made by Ohio Tool Company. Ohio Tool ceased making planes about 1917. The later planes, made by a different supplier, are similar to the early variety except for the marking mentioned above. They also have minor differences in chamfering and shape of the wedges. The differences are difficult to discern without having both types available for comparison.

Wooden planes of this type were designated in the catalogs as KS, KHS, etc. These letters were for ordering purposes only and do not appear on the hardware.

The following planes were listed:

KS Wooden Smooth Plane

KS Wooden Smooth Plane $35 - $60
Offered: 1906 thru 1929
Material: Beechwood
Length: 8 inches
Width of Cutter: 2, 2 1/8, 2 1/4 inches
Type of Cutter: Double
Front Knob: Ebonized 1906 thru 1917, Walnut 1918 and later
Logo: Wedge & Bar
These were general purpose smoothing planes used to prepare the surface of a workpiece. They were short to allow usage on a small surface. The throat was normally narrow and the cutter was set for a fine shaving

KHS Wooden Smooth Plane, handled

KHS Wooden Smooth Plane, Handled $45 - $70
    Offered: 1906 thru 1929
    Material: Beechwood
    Length: 10 1/2 inches 1906, 9 1/2 inches 1907 and later
    Width of Cutter: 2, 2 1/8, 2 1/4 inches
    Type of Cutter: Double
    Front Knob: Ebonized 1906 thru 1917, Walnut 1918 and later
    Logo: Wedge & Bar
    These were general purpose smoothing planes used to prepare the sur-
face of a workpiece. The handled variety was easier to use especially for
long periods. They were short to allow usage on a small surface. The throat
was normally narrow and the cutter was set for a fine shaving

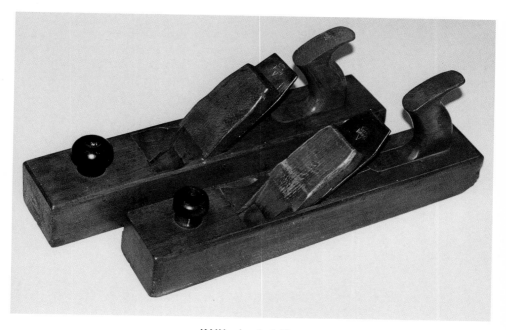

KJ Wooden Jack Plane

KJ Wooden Jack Plane $30 - $55
    Offered: 1906 thru 1929
    Material: Beechwood
    Length: 15 inches 1906 & 1910 and later, 16 inches 1907 thru 1909
    Width of Cutter: 2 1/8, 2 1/4 inches
    Type of Cutter: Double
    Front Knob: Ebonized 1906 thru 1917, Walnut 1918 and later
    Logo: Wedge & Bar
    The jack plane is the workhorse of the plane family. It is a convenient middle
size and is used for any and all bench plane functions. This size is one of
the most common of Keen Kutter planes
    The illustration shows one jack plane with an walnut front knob and a
similar one with an ebonized knob. The walnut variety is relatively scarce

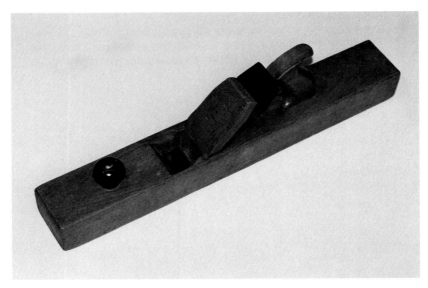

KF Wooden Fore Plane.
Similar to KP 26, KP 28, KP 30

KF Wooden Fore Plane $40 - $70
> Offered: 1906 thru 1929
> Material: Beechwood
> Length: 20 inches 1906 & 1910 and later, 22 inches 1907 thru 1909. A 24 inch plane has been noted
> Width of Cutter: 2 3/8, 2 1/2 inches
> Type of Cutter: Double
> Front Knob: Ebonized 1906 thru 1917, Walnut 1918 and later
> Logo: Wedge & Bar
> The fore plane is actually a short jointer. It is sometimes used before the jointer plane allowing the jointer to be kept extra sharp to make the final cut for edge joining

KP 26 Wooden Jointer Plane $45 - $75
> Offered: 1906 thru 1929
> Material: Beechwood
> Length: 26 inches
> Width of Cutter: 2 1/2, 2 5/8 inches
> Type of Cutter: Double
> Front Knob: Ebonized 1906 thru 1917, Walnut 1918 and later
> Logo: Wedge & Bar
> See KF Wooden Fore Plane illustration
> The jointer is the longest of the bench plane family. It is used where maximum accuracy is desired. Its extra length and weight reduces waviness to a minimum. The KP26 is a short version of a jointer

KP 28, KP 30 Wooden Jointer Plane $60 - $85
   Offered: 1906 thru 1917
   Material: Beechwood
   Length: 28, 30 inches
   Width of Cutter: 2 1/2, 2 5/8 inches each length
   Type of Cutter: Double
   Front Knob: Ebonized
   Logo: Wedge & Bar, St. Louis U.S.A.
   See KF Wooden Fore Plane illustration
   The jointer is the longest of the bench plane family. It is used where maximum accuracy is desired. Its extra length and weight reduces waviness to a minimum

KRJ Wooden Jack Plane, Razee

KRJ Wooden Jack Plane, Razee $40 - $65
   Offered: 1910 thru 1915
   Material: Beechwood
   Length: 15 inches
   Width of Cutter: 2 1/8, 2 1/4 inches
   Type of Cutter: Double
   Front Knob: Ebonized
   Logo: Wedge & Bar, St. Louis U.S.A.
   The razee jack plane is identical in function to the common wooden jack plane except for the lowered position of the rear handle. It has better balance than the common jack and is somewhat easier to use. Razee planes never became popular and are therefore relatively scarce

KRF Wooden Fore Plane, Razee

KRF Wooden Fore Plane, Razee $50 - $75
   Offered: 1910 thru 1917
   Material: Beechwood
   Length: 20 inches
   Width of Cutter: 2 3/8, 2 1/2 inches
   Type of Cutter: Double
   Front Knob: Ebonized
   Logo: Wedge & Bar, St. Louis U.S.A.
   The razee fore plane is identical in function to the common wooden fore plane except for the lowered position of the rear handle. It has better balance than the common fore plane and is somewhat easier to use. Razee planes never became popular and are therefore relatively scarce

KRP 26 Wooden Jointer Plane, Razee

KRP 26 Wooden Jointer Plane, Razee $60 - $90
  Offered: 1910 thru 1917
  Material: Beechwood
  Length: 26 inches
  Width of Cutter: 2 1/2, 2 5/8 inches
  Type of Cutter: Double
  Front Knob: Ebonized
  Logo: Wedge & Bar, St. Louis U.S.A.
  The razee jointer plane is identical in function to the common wooden jointer plane except for the lowered position of the rear handle. It has better balance than the common jointer and is somewhat easier to use. Razee planes never became popular and are therefore relatively scarce

Keen Kutter Planes "KK"

Simmons Hardware Company announced a line of metal and wood bottom planes in a 1906 brochure No. 523. They were designated with "KK" and the plane number. This series of planes were all coated with black enamel except as noted in the detail descriptions here-in. They were fitted with Keen Kutter irons (cutters) which had been sharpened and hand whetted on an oilstone. The cutters were incised with the wedge & bar logo with the words St. Louis U.S.A. inside of the logo outline. Each plane was packed in a separate cardboard box.

The planes appear to be identical in construction to the planes offered by Ohio Tool Company in their own catalogs. There is little doubt that Ohio Tool made the planes for Simmons.

Many of the catalog illustrations show the Keen Kutter logo and/or the words Keen Kutter on the sides of the planes. The metal planes were not marked on the sides; however, several wood bottom planes have been observed with a logo incised on the side of the wood portion.

This section contains a listing, in numerical order, of all metal planes, wood bottom planes, routers and scrapers offered from 1906 thru 1912

Early "KK" Planes

Several Keen Kutter planes with non-standard markings on the castings have been noted. Markings are non-standard in the sense that they differ from most KK series planes and also from the catalog illustrations. Metal bench planes, wood bottom planes and four sizes of block planes have been observed. The cutters in some of these planes are also unique. In some cases they have the semi-circular saw-tooth mark, others have a wedge & bar mark, and in other cases the marking is merely the words *Keen Kutter*.

The metal bench planes are marked with KK and No along with the size number. See illustration. The lever caps are unpainted. In most cases the lateral adjust levers are the type with a turned-up end rather than a disc. The cutters are tapered and thick.

Early Metal Bench Plane markings

Early Wood Bottom Plane marking

The toe ends of wood bottom planes are marked No. and the plane number, i.e. No. 29. The markings are uneven and appear to have been made with individual letter and number stamps. See illustration. They also have the semi-circular saw-tooth or the wedge & bar mark on the toe. The lever caps are unpainted. In most cases the lateral adjust levers are the type with a turned-up end rather than a disc. The lever caps are polished. The cutters are tapered and thick.

The early block planes have KK on the front part of the casting and the plane number at the rear. See illustration.

Planes with these unique markings are not shown in any available Simmons Hardware Company catalog. It is assumed that they are the forerunners of the KK series announced in the 1906 brochure. Use of the saw-tooth logo (1895-1905) indicates that they were manufactured or at least contracted prior to adoption of the wedge & bar logo in early 1905. It is probable that they were made during the fist year of production. They were made by the Ohio Tool Company.

These planes are relatively scarce compared to the standard variety and command a premium price compared to the standard tool of the same size.

Early Block Plane marking

"KK" Bench Planes - Metal

The "KK" series bench planes numbered KK3 thru KK8C are the family of flat bottom planes used for general purpose smoothing and fitting and for reducing stock size. KK and the plane number are embossed forward of the front knob. The double cutters are extra thick and are said to reduce chattering when working hard or knotty wood. The cutters are incised with the wedge & bar logo. The planes are finished with black enamel except for the sides and the lever caps which are polished.

Each plane is fitted with lateral adjustment provisions. The lateral adjust lever was formed by a one-half twist at the upper end. Knobs and handles are made of rosewood. The knobs are short. Hold-down bolts for the knobs and handles are made of steel. The planes numbered with a C have corrugated bottoms. The lengthwise corrugations are said to make the plane slide easier especially on resinous woods. The letter C does not appear on the part.

There are not any size 1, 2 or 5 1/4 planes in this series.

KK3 Smooth Plane $60 - $85
Offered: 1906 thru 1912
Length: 8 inches, 8 3/4 inches observed not including the rear handle over-
hang
Width of Cutter: 1 3/4 inches
Type of Cutter: Double, extra heavy
Knob and Handle: Rosewood
Lever Cap: Polished, no marking
Logo on the Cutter: Wedge & Bar, St. Louis U.S.A.
KK3 embossed forward of the front knob
See KK4 Smooth Plane illustration
The KK3 is a general purpose smoothing plane appropriate for use on a small workpiece or in a cabinet shop. This tool was also used in many tool kits where space was limited.

KK3C Smooth Plane $60 - $85
Offered: 1906 thru 1912
Same as KK3 except that this tool has a corrugated bottom instead of a smooth bottom
See KK4 Smooth Plane illustration

KK4 Smooth Plane.
Similar to KK3, KK3C, KK4C, KK4 1/2, KK4 1/2C

KK4 Smooth Plane $40 - $65
Offered: 1906 thru 1912
Length: 9 inches

Width of Cutter: 2 inches
Type of Cutter: Double, extra heavy
Knob and Handle: Rosewood
Lever Cap: Polished, no marking
Logo on the Cutter: Wedge & Bar, St. Louis U.S.A.
KK4 embossed forward of the front knob
The KK4 is a general purpose smoothing plane used for smoothing the face of workpiece and for fitting small articles. The throat is normally set narrow for a fine shaving. The four size is one of the most common of Keen Kutter planes

KK4C Smooth Plane $40 - $65
Offered: 1906 thru 1912
Same as KK4 except that this tool has a corrugated bottom instead of a smooth bottom
See KK4 Smooth Plane illustration

KK4 1/2 marking

KK4 1/2 Smooth Plane $50 - $85
Offered: 1906 thru 1912
Length: 10 inches
Width of Cutter: 2 3/8 inches
Type of Cutter: Double, extra heavy
Knob and Handle: Rosewood
Lever Cap: Polished, no marking
Logo on the Cutter: Wedge & Bar, St. Louis U.S.A.
KK4 1/2 embossed forward of the front knob
See KK4 Smooth Plane illustration
The KK4 1/2 is intended for a workman who prefers a slightly wider and heavier smooth plane. Spacing of the size marking on this plane sometimes leads to confusion. Auction bills often list this plane as a KK42. See illustration

KK4 1/2C Smooth Plane $50 - $85
Offered: 1906 thru 1912
Same as KK4 1/2 except that this tool has a corrugated bottom instead of a smooth bottom.
See KK4 Smooth Plane illustration

KK5 Jack Plane $40 - $65
Offered: 1906 thru 1912
Length: 14 inches
Width of Cutter: 2 inches
Type of Cutter: Double, extra heavy
Knob and Handle: Rosewood
Lever Cap: Polished, no marking
Logo on the Cutter: Wedge & Bar, St. Louis U.S.A.
KK5 embossed forward of the front knob

See KK5 1/2 Jack Plane illustration
The jack plane is the workhorse of the plane family. It is a convenient middle size and is used for any and all bench plane functions. The five is one of the most common of Keen Kutter planes

KK5C Jack Plane $40 - $65
  Offered: 1906 thru 1912
  Same as KK5 except that this tool has a corrugated bottom instead of a smooth bottom.
  See KK5 1/2 Jack Plane illustration

KK 5 1/2 Jack Plane.
Similar to KK5, KK5C, KK5 1/2C, KK6, KK6C, KK7, KK7C, KK8, KK8C

KK5 1/2 marking

KK5 1/2 Jack Plane $50 - $75
  Offered: 1906 thru 1912
  Length: 15 inches
  Width of Cutter: 2 1/4 inches
  Type of Cutter: Double, extra heavy
  Knob and Handle: Rosewood
  Lever Cap: Polished, no marking
  Logo on the Cutter: Wedge & Bar, St. Louis U.S.A.
  KK5 1/2 embossed forward of the front knob
  The KK5 1/2 is intended for a workman who prefers a slightly wider and heavier jack plane. Spacing of the size marking on this plane sometimes leads to confusion. See illustration

KK5 1/2C Jack Plane $50 - $75
  Offered: 1906 thru 1912
  Same as KK5 1/2 except that this tool has a corrugated bottom instead of a smooth bottom.
  See KK5 1/2 Jack Plane illustration

KK6 Fore Plane $45 - $70
  Offered: 1906 thru 1912
  Length: 18 inches. 17 5/8 inches observed
  Width of Cutter: 2 3/8 inches
  Type of Cutter: Double, extra heavy
  Knob and Handle: Rosewood
  Lever Cap: Polished, no marking
  Logo on the Cutter: Wedge & Bar, St. Louis

U.S.A.
KK6 embossed forward of the front knob
See KK5 1/2 Jack Plane illustration
The KK6 Fore plane is actually a short jointer. It is sometimes used before
the jointer plane allowing the jointer to be kept extra sharp to make the final
cut for edge joining

KK6C Fore Plane $45 - $70
Offered: 1906 thru 1912
Same as KK6 except that this tool has a corrugated bottom instead of a
smooth bottom
See KK5 1/2 Jack Plane illustration

KK7 Jointer Plane $50 - $75
Offered: 1906 thru 1912
Length: 22 inches
Width of Cutter: 2 3/8 inches
Type of Cutter: Double, extra heavy
Knob and Handle: Rosewood
Lever Cap: Polished, no marking
Logo on the Cutter: Wedge & Bar, St. Louis U.S.A.
KK7 embossed forward of the front knob
See KK5 1/2 Jack Plane illustration
The KK7 Jointer is used for edge joining of long boards and for final trim-
ming of long workpieces such as doors

KK7C Jointer Plane $50 - $75
Offered: 1906 thru 1912
Same as KK7 except that this tool has a corrugated bottom instead of a
smooth bottom
See KK5 1/2 Jack Plane illustration

KK8 Jointer Plane $55 - $80
Offered: 1906 thru 1912
Length: 24 inches
Width of Cutter: 2 5/8 inches
Type of Cutter: Double, extra heavy
Knob and Handle: Rosewood
Lever Cap: Polished, no marking
Logo on the Cutter: Wedge & Bar, St. Louis U.S.A.
KK8 embossed forward of the front knob
See KK5 1/2 Jack Plane illustration
The KK8 Jointer is the longest of the metal planes in this series and is used
where maximum accuracy is desired. Its extra length and weight reduces
waviness to a minimum

KK8C Jointer Plane $55 - $80
Offered: 1906 thru 1912
Same as KK8 except that this tool has a corrugated bottom instead of a
smooth bottom
See KK5 1/2 Jack Plane illustration

KK9 1/2 Block Plane. Similar to KK15

KK9 1/2 Block Plane $40 - $60
Offered: 1906 thru 1912
Length: 6 inches. 6 1/4 inches observed
Width of Cutter: 1 3/4 inches. 1 5/8 and 1 9/16 inches observed
Logo on the Cutter: Wedge & Bar, St. Louis U.S.A.
KK9 1/2 embossed just forward of the cutter adjust screw. Examples have been noted that are marked forward of the front knob. See illustration
Has screw and lateral adjustment of the cutter and throat adjustment provisions
The KK9 1/2 is a fully adjustable general purpose block plane.

KK9 3/4 Block Plane

KK9 3/4 Block Plane $375 - $450
Offered: 1906 thru 1912
Length: 6 inches. 6 1/4 inches ob-
served
Width of Cutter: 1 3/4 inches.
1 9/16 inches observed
Handle: Rosewood
Logo on the Cutter: Wedge & Bar,
St. Louis U.S.A.
KK9 3/4 embossed forward of the
front knob

Has screw and lateral adjustment of the cutter and throat adjustment provisions. The KK9 3/4 is the same as the KK9 1/2 except for the rear handle
The handle and handle attachment were often damaged during use. Beware of repaired or replaced parts

KK10 Carriage Maker's Rabbet Plane. Similar to KK10 1/2

KK10 Carriage Maker's Rabbet Plane $175 - $250
    Offered: 1906 thru 1912
    Length: 13 inches
    Width of Cutter: 2 1/8 inches
    Type of Cutter: Double, extra heavy
    Knob and Handle: Rosewood
    Lever Cap: Polished, no marking
    Logo on the Cutter: Wedge & Bar, St. Louis U.S.A.
    KK10 embossed forward of the front knob
    Has screw and lateral adjustment of the cutter. The lateral adjust lever
    was formed by a one half twist at the upper end

KK10 1/2 Rabbet Plane with adjustable throat

KK10 1/2 Carriage Maker's Rabbet Plane $200 - $300
    Offered: 1906 thru 1912
    Length: 9 inches including the rear handle overhang
    Width of Cutter: 2 1/8 inches. 1 3/4 inches observed
    Type of Cutter: Double, extra heavy

Knob and Handle: Rosewood
Lever Cap: Polished, no marking
Logo on the Cutter: Wedge & Bar, St. Louis U.S.A.
KK10 1/2 embossed forward of the rear handle
See KK10 Carriage Maker's Rabbet Plane illustration
Has screw and lateral adjustment of the cutter. The lateral adjust lever
was formed by a one half twist at the upper end
The earliest type of the KK10 1/2 has an adjustable throat. The adjust-
ment is made by loosening the front knob. This earlier type is scarce and
commands a higher price than the later variety

KK15 Block Plane $60 - $85
    Offered: 1906 thru 1912
    Length: 7 inches
    Width of Cutter: 1 3/4 inches
    Logo on the Cutter: Wedge & Bar, St. Louis U.S.A.
    KK15 embossed forward of the front knob
    Same as the KK9 1/2 except for size
    See KK9 1/2 Block Plane illustration
    Has screw and lateral adjustment of the cutter and throat adjustment
    provisions

KK18 Block Plane, knuckle joint. Similar to KK19

KK18 Block Plane, Knuckle Joint $45 - $70
    Offered: 1906 thru 1912
    Length: 6 inches. 6 1/4 inches observed
    Width of Cutter: 1 3/4 inches. 1 5/8 inches observed
    Finish: Nickel plated trimmings
    Logo on the Cutter: Wedge & Bar, St. Louis U.S.A.
    KK18 embossed forward of the front knob

Has screw and lateral adjustment of the cutter and throat adjustment provisions
A later model is identical except that the lever cap is incised Keen Kutter.
See illustration

KK19 Block Plane, Knuckle Joint $55 - $80
 Offered: 1906 thru 1912
 Length: 7 inches
 Width of Cutter: 1 3/4 inches
 KK19 embossed forward of the front knob
 Same as the KK18 except for length.
 See KK18 Block Plane, Knuckle Joint illustration

"KK" Bench Planes - Wood Bottom

The "KK" series of wood bottom bench planes, numbered KK23 thru KK36, are the family of flat bottom planes used for general purpose smoothing and fitting and for reducing stock size. The double cutters are extra thick and said to reduce chattering when working hard or knotty wood. The cutters are incised with the wedge and bar logo. The metal portions of the planes are finished with black enamel. The catalog descriptive material states that the lever caps are polished; however, the caps noted on this series of planes are painted black.

Each plane is fitted with lateral adjustment provisions. The lateral adjust lever is formed by a one half twist at the upper end. Knobs, handles and bottoms are made of beechwood. Hold-down bolts for the knobs and handles are made of steel. The wood bottoms are made of thoroughly seasoned blocks coated with a solution which prevents warping.

The wood bottoms of these planes are subject to wear and cracking. In many cases the bottoms have been dressed down by the user to maintain squareness or by a tool dealer for the sake of appearance. In some cases the longer varieties have been cut off so that they will fit into a chicken box. Any modification or excessive deterioration greatly reduces value.

There are not any size 22, 25, 27 1/2 or 34 planes in this series.

KK23 Smooth Plane, wood bottom. Similar to KK24

KK23 Smooth Plane, Wood Bottom $35 - $55
 Offered: 1906 thru 1912
 Length: 9 inches
 Width of Cutter:1 3/4 inches
 Type of Cutter: Double, extra heavy
 Wood parts: Beechwood
 Lever Cap: No marking
 Logo on the Cutter: Wedge & Bar, St. Louis U.S.A.
 KK23 and the logo are incised on the left side of the wood bottom

KK24 Smooth Plane, Wood Bottom $35 - $55
    Offered: 1906 thru 1912
    Length: 8 inches
    Width of Cutter: 2 inches
    Type of Cutter: Double, extra heavy
    Wood parts: Beechwood
    Lever Cap: No marking
    Logo on the Cutter: Wedge & Bar, St. Louis U.S.A.
    KK24 and the logo are incised on the left side of the wood bottom
    See KK23 Smooth Plane, Wood Bottom illustration

KK26 Jack Plane, wood bottom. Similar to KK27, KK28, KK29, KK30, KK31, KK32, KK33

KK26 Jack Plane, Wood Bottom $35 - $55
    Offered: 1906 thru 1912
    Length: 15 inches
    Width of Cutter: 2 inches
    Type of Cutter: Double, extra heavy
    Wood parts: Beechwood
    Lever Cap: No marking
    Logo on the Cutter: Wedge & Bar, St. Louis U.S.A.
    KK26 and the logo are incised on the top surface of the plane forward of
    the knob

KK27 Jack Plane, Wood Bottom $35 - $55
    Offered: 1906 thru 1912
    Length: 15 inches
    Width of Cutter: 2 1/8 inches
    Type of Cutter: Double, extra heavy
    Wood parts: Beechwood
    Lever Cap: No marking
    Logo on the Cutter: Wedge & Bar, St. Louis U.S.A.
    KK27 and the logo are incised on the top surface of the plane forward of
    the knob
    See KK26 Jack Plane, Wood Bottom illustration

KK28 Fore Plane, Wood Bottom $35 - $55
    Offered: 1906 thru 1912
    Length: 18 inches
    Width of Cutter: 2 3/8 inches

Type of Cutter: Double, extra heavy
Wood parts: Beechwood
Lever Cap: No marking
Logo on the Cutter: Wedge & Bar, St. Louis U.S.A.
KK28 and the logo are incised on the top surface of the plane forward of the knob
See KK26 Jack Plane, Wood Bottom illustration

KK29 Fore Plane, Wood Bottom $40 - $60
Offered: 1906 thru 1912
Length: 20 inches
Width of Cutter: 2 3/8 inches
Type of Cutter: Double, extra heavy
Wood parts: Beechwood
Lever Cap: No marking
Logo on the Cutter: Wedge & Bar, St. Louis U.S.A.
KK29 and the logo are incised on the top surface of the plane forward of the knob
See KK26 Jack Plane, Wood Bottom illustration

KK30 Jointer Plane, Wood Bottom $40 - $60
Offered: 1906 thru 1912
Length: 22 inches
Width of Cutter: 2 3/8 inches
Type of Cutter: Double, extra heavy
Wood parts: Beechwood
Lever Cap: No marking
Logo on the Cutter: Wedge & Bar, St. Louis U.S.A.
KK30 and the logo are incised on the top surface of the plane forward of the knob
See KK26 Jack Plane, Wood Bottom illustration

KK31 Jointer Plane, Wood Bottom $40 - $60
Offered: 1906 thru 1912
Length: 24 inches
Width of Cutter: 2 3/8 inches
Type of Cutter: Double, extra heavy
Wood parts: Beechwood
Lever Cap: No marking
Logo on the Cutter: Wedge & Bar, St. Louis U.S.A.
KK31 and the logo are incised on the top surface of the plane forward of the knob
See KK26 Jack Plane, Wood Bottom illustration

KK32 Jointer Plane, Wood Bottom $40 - $60
Offered: 1906 thru 1912
Length: 26 inches
Width of Cutter: 2 5/8 inches
Type of Cutter: Double, extra heavy
Wood parts: Beechwood
Lever Cap: No marking
Logo on the Cutter: Wedge & Bar, St. Louis U.S.A.

KK32 and the logo are incised on the top surface of the plane forward of the knob
See KK26 Jack Plane, Wood Bottom illustration

KK33 Jointer Plane, Wood Bottom $45 - $65
    Offered: 1906 thru 1912
    Length: 28 inches
    Width of Cutter: 2 5/8 inches
    Type of Cutter: Double, extra heavy
    Wood parts: Beechwood
    Lever Cap: No marking
    Logo on the Cutter: Wedge & Bar, St. Louis U.S.A.
    KK33 and the logo are incised on the top surface of the plane forward of the knob
    See KK26 Jack Plane, Wood Bottom illustration

KK35 Smooth Plane, handled, wood bottom. Similar to KK36

KK35 Smooth Plane, Handled, Wood Bottom $35 - $55
    Offered: 1906 thru 1912
    Length: 9 inches. 8 11/16 inches observed
    Width of Cutter: 2 inches
    Type of Cutter: Double, extra heavy
    Wood parts: Beechwood
    Lever Cap: No marking
    Logo on the Cutter: Wedge & Bar, St. Louis U.S.A.
    KK35 and the logo are incised on the left side of the wood bottom

KK36 Smooth Plane, Handled, Wood Bottom $35 - $55
    Offered: 1906 thru 1912
    Length: 10 inches. 9 inches observed
    Width of Cutter: 2 3/8 inches
    Type of Cutter: Double, extra heavy
    Wood parts: Beechwood
    Lever Cap: No marking
    Logo on the Cutter: Wedge & Bar, St. Louis U.S.A.
    KK36 and the logo are incised on the left side of the wood bottom
    See KK35 Smooth Plane, Handled, Wood Bottom illustration

KK60 Block Plane, low angle

KK60 Block Plane, Low Angle $45 - $85
    Offered: 1906 thru 1912
    Length: 6 inches. 6 1/8 inches observed
    Width of Cutter: 1 1/2 inches. 1 3/8 inches observed
    Finish: Nickel plated lever cap
    Logo on the Cutter: Wedge & Bar, St. Louis U.S.A.
    KK60 embossed on the aft end of the casting. Another variety has KK60
        embossed on the forward end of the casting.
    Has screw adjustment of the cutter and throat adjustment provisions.
    The screw adjustment mechanism swivels to accomplish lateral adjustment

KK65 Block Plane, low angle

KK65 Block Plane, Low Angle $45 - $85
    Offered: 1906 thru 1912
    Length: 7 inches
    Width of Cutter: 1 3/4 inches
    Finish: Nickel plated lever cap. Japanned
        lever cap observed
    Logo on the Cutter: Wedge & Bar, St.
        Louis U.S.A.
    KK65 embossed forward of the front
    knob. Another variety has KK65 embossed on the aft end of the casting
    Has screw adjustment of the cutter and
    throat adjustment provisions. The screw
    adjustment mechanism swivels to accomplish lateral adjustment

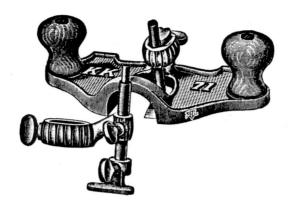

KK71 Router, open throat

KK71 Router, Open Throat $110 - $150
Offered: 1906 thru 1912
Length: 7 1/2 inches
Cutters: Two provided, 1/4 and 1/2 inches
Knobs: Rosewood
Finish: Nickel plated
KK71 embossed on the casting
Cutters are not marked
An attachment is provided that can be used to close the throat
Hold down screws for the knobs are made of steel
The latest model has a worm nut for use in fine adjustment of the cutter.
See illustration. The cutters provided with this model are notched
The hole in the casting, shown in the upper photo, was added by the user

KK75 Rabbet plane, bull nose

KK75 Rabbet Plane, Bull Nose $125 - $175
  Offered: 1906 thru 1912
  Length: 4 inches
  Width of Cutter: 1inch
  Logo on the Cutter: Wedge & Bar, St. Louis U.S.A.
  KK75 embossed on the top surface aft of the cutter
  Not adjustable

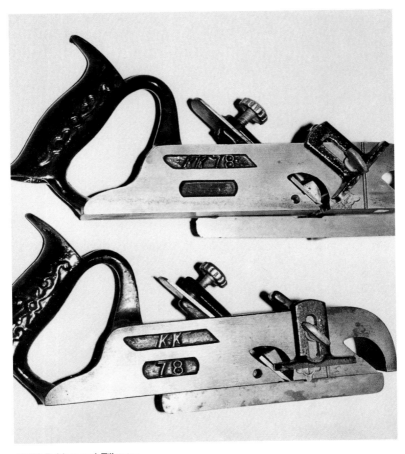

KK78 Rabbet and Filletster

KK78 Rabbet and Filletster

KK78 Rabbet and Filletster $100 - $175
>   Offered: 1906 thru 1912
>   Length: 8 1/2 inches (base)
>   Width of Cutter: 1 1/2 inches
>   Logo on the Cutter: Wedge & Bar, St. Louis U.S.A.
>   KK78 embossed on the right side of the casting. Two variations of marking
>   are noted, see illustrations
>   A right hand spur, depth stop and adjustable fence are provided. The cast-
>   ing is machined flat on both sides.
>   The plane can be used as a right or left hand rabbet or as a bull nose
>   rabbet.

KK79 Cabinet Scraper

KK79 Cabinet Scraper $40 - $90
>   Offered: 1907 thru 1912
>   Length: 11 inches
>   Width of Blade: 2 3/4 inches
>   Finish: Nickel plated 1912 only
>   Logo on the Blade: Wedge & Bar, St. Louis U.S.A.
>   KK79 embossed on the casting
>   Holes in both handles
>   The nickel plated variety is relatively scarce

KK80 Cabinet Scraper

KK80 Cabinet Scraper $55 - $90
    Offered: 1906 only
    Length: 11 inches
    Width of Blade: 2 3/4 inches. 2 13/16 inches observed
    Logo on the Blade: Wedge & Bar, St. Louis U.S.A.
    KK80 embossed on the casting
    Holes in both handles

KK102 Block Plane

KK102 Block Plane $30 - $45
    Offered: 1906 thru 1912
    Length: 5 1/2 inches
    Width of Cutter: 1 1/4 inches
    Logo on the Cutter: Wedge & Bar, St. Louis U.S.A.
    KK102 embossed aft of the cutter
    Not adjustable

KK103 Block Plane

KK103 Block Plane $30 - $45
    Offered: 1906 thru 1912
    Length: 5 1/2 inches. 5 7/16 inches observed
    Width of Cutter: 1 1/4 inches
    Logo on the Cutter: Wedge & Bar, St. Louis U.S.A.
    KK103 embossed aft of the cutter
    Lever adjustment of the cutter
    The KK103 is one of the most common of Keen Kutter planes

KK110 Block Plane

KK110 Block Plane $35 - $60
    Offered: 1906 thru 1912
    Length: 7 1/2 inches. 7 1/8 inches observed
    Width of Cutter: 1 3/4 inches. 1 5/8 inches observed
    Knob: Stained hardwood
    Logo on the Cutter: Wedge & Bar, St. Louis U.S.A.
    KK110 embossed aft of the cutter
    Another variety is marked forward of the knob. See illustration
    Not adjustable
    The KK110 is one of the most common of Keen Kutter planes

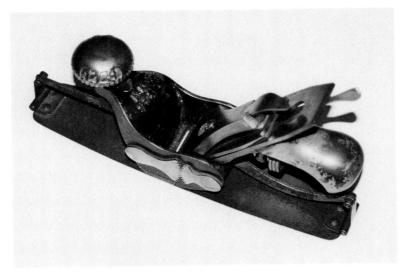

KK113 Circular Plane

KK113 Circular Plane $300 - $450
 Offered: 1906 only
 Length: 10 inches. 10 1/8 inches observed
 Width of Cutter: 1 3/4 inches
 Type of Cutter: Double, extra heavy
 Lever Cap: Polished, no marking
 Finish: Rear handle and front knob are nickel plated
 Logo on the Cutter: Wedge & Bar, St. Louis U.S.A.
 KK113 embossed on the adjustment knob and on the casting just aft of the knob
 Screw and lateral adjustment of the cutter. The lateral adjust lever was formed by a one half twist at the upper end. The lower end of the lever has the older type bent-up tab rather than a disk
 The flexible steel sole allows the plane to be used on either a concave or convex surface

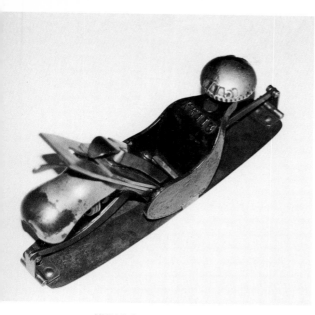

KK115 Circular Plane
$250 - $400

Offered: 1907 thru 1912

Length: 10 inches. 10 1/8 inches observed

Width of Cutter: 1 3/4 inches

Type of Cutter: Double, extra heavy

Lever Cap: Polished, no marking

Finish: Rear handle and front knob are nickel plated

Logo on the Cutter: Wedge & Bar, St. Louis U.S.A.

KK115 Circular Plane

KK115 embossed on the adjustment knob and on the casting just aft of the knob

Screw and lateral adjustment of the cutter. The lateral adjust lever was formed by a one half twist at the upper end

The flexible steel sole allows the plane to be used on either a concave or convex surface

KK120 Block Plane $35 - $60

Offered: 1906 thru 1912

Length: 7 1/2 inches. 7 1/8 inches observed

Width of Cutter: 1 3/4 inches per catalog. 1 5/8 inches observed

Knob: Stained hardwood

Logo on the Cutter: Wedge & Bar, St. Louis U.S.A.

KK120 embossed aft of the cutter. Another variety is marked forward of the knob. See illustration

Lever adjustment of the cutter

One KK120 has been observed with the words Keen Kutter rather than the logo incised on the cutter. This variety of cutter is not shown in any Simmons catalog

A 1 3/4 inch cutter would not fit within the casting on the planes observed. A catalog error is assumed

KK120 Block Plane

KK130 Block Plane, Double Ender

KK130 Block Plane, Double Ender $75 - $100
    Offered: 1906 thru 1912
    Length: 8 inches. 7 7/8 inches observed
    Width of Cutter: 1 3/4 inches. 1 5/8 inches observed
    Knob: Rosewood
    Logo on the Cutter: Wedge & Bar, St. Louis U.S.A.
    KK130 embossed forward of the knob
    Not adjustable
    The two cutter seats allow the plane to be used for either regular or bull nose work
    Some catalogs list the length of this plane as 6 inches. This is considered to be a catalog error

KK140 Rabbet and Block Plane

KK140 Rabbet and Block Plane $250 - $400
    Offered: 1906 thru 1912
    Length: 7 inches
    Width of Cutter: 1 3/4 inches. 1 5/8 inches observed
    Knob: Fruitwood
    Logo on the Cutter: Wedge & Bar, St. Louis U.S.A.
    KK140 embossed forward of the knob
    Lever adjustment of the cutter
    A unique feature of this plane is that the end of the adjustment lever is formed into an elongated sphere. The sphere is about 5/16 inches in diameter
    This plane was quite subject to breakage during use and is therefore scarce

KK171 1/2 Router, Closed Throat

KK171 1/2 Router, Closed Throat $100 - $150
  Offered: 1907 thru 1912
  Length: 7 5/8 inches
  Knobs: Rosewood. An early model with beechwood knobs has been observed
  Cutters: Two provided, 1/4 and 1/2 inch
  Finish: Nickel plated
  KK171 1/2 embossed on the casting
  The two bosses that appear to be for attachment of a fence are not drilled. A fence is not mentioned in the catalog descriptions.
  Hold down screws for the knobs are made of steel
  The cutters are not marked
  The latest model has a worm nut that can be used for fine adjustment of the cutter. See illustration. The cutters on this model are notched

KK190 Rabbet Plane. Similar to KK191, KK192

KK190 Rabbet Plane $175 - $225
> Offered: 1906 thru 1912
> Length: 8 inches
> Width of Cutter: 1 1/2 inches
> Logo on the Cutter: Wedge & Bar, St. Louis U.S.A.
> KK190 embossed on the left side of the casting. Two variations of marking have been noted
> Not adjustable. A right hand spur and depth stop are provided. Both sides of the casting are machined flat so that the plane can be used as either a right or left hand rabbet

KK191 Rabbet Plane $175 - $225
> Offered: 1907 thru 1912
> Length: 8 inches
> Width of Cutter: 1 1/4 inches
> Logo on the Cutter: Wedge & Bar, St. Louis U.S.A.
> KK191 embossed on the left side of the casting. Two variations of marking have been noted
> See KK190 Rabbet Plane illustration
> Same as the K190 Rabbet Plane except for width of the cutter

KK192 Rabbet Plane $175 - $225
> Offered: 1907 thru 1912
> Length: 8 inches
> Width of Cutter: 1 inch
> Logo on the Cutter: Wedge & Bar, St. Louis U.S.A.
> KK192 embossed on the left side of the casting. Two variations of marking have been noted
> See KK190 Rabbet Plane illustration

KK212 Veneer Scraper

KK212 Veneer Scraper $175 - $250
> Offered: 1907 thru 1912
> Length: 5 3/4 inches
> Width of Blade: 3 inches
> Logo on the Blade: Wedge & Bar, St. Louis U.S.A.
> KK212 embossed on the casting forward of the blade
> The angle of the blade is adjustable

KK220 Block Plane $40 - $75
> Offered: 1906 thru 1912
> Length: 7 1/2 inches
> Width of Cutter: 1 3/4 inches
> Knob: Hardwood
> Logo on the Cutter: Wedge & Bar, St. Louis U.S.A.
> KK220 embossed forward of the knob
> Screw adjustment of the cutter. The screw adjustment mechanism swivels
to accomplish lateral adjustment

KK220 Block Plane

KK240 Scrub Plane

KK240 Scrub Plane $120 - $175
> Offered: 1907 thru 1912
> Length: 9 1/2 inches
> Width of Cutter: 1 1/4 inches
> Type of Cutter: Single, extra heavy
> Knob and Handle: Beechwood
> Logo on the Cutter: Wedge & Bar, St. Louis U.S.A.

KK240 embossed forward of the knob
Not adjustable
Lever cap and sides are painted black as well as the inside of the base.
This plane is intended to be used for roughing down work before the use
of the jack or other plane. The cutter has a rounded cutting edge

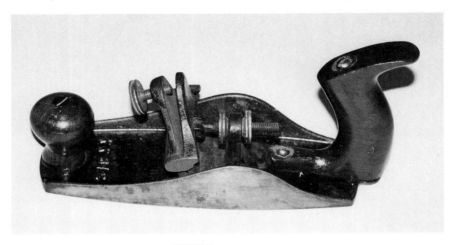

KK312 Scraper

KK312 Scraper $250 - $350
    Offered: 1907 thru 1912
    Length: 9 inches
    Width of Blade: 3 inches per catalog
    Handle and Knob: Rosewood
    Logo on the Blade: Wedge & Bar, St. Louis U.S.A.
    KK312 embossed behind the front knob
    The angle of the blade is adjustable. Hold down screws for the knob and
    handle are made of steel.
    The opening for the blade is slightly less than 3 inches

KKC Cabinet Scraper

KKC Cabinet Scraper $25 - $40
    Offered: 1906 thru 1911
    Sizes: 2 x 4 inches, 2 1/2 x 5 inches, 3 x 5 inches, 3 1/2 x 6 inches, and 4
       x 6 inches
    Logo: Wedge & Bar, St. Louis U.S.A.
    These are flat steel scrapers without handles. Polished and tempered
    Neither the catalog number nor the size is shown on the hardware

Keen Kutter Planes "K"

The 1913 Simmons Hardware Company general catalog and a Simmons brochure No. 1548 listed a new line of metal and wood bottom planes designated with a single "K" in front of the plane number. The number is included on the plane. This series of planes are coated with black enamel except as noted in the detail descriptions here-in. They were fitted with Keen Kutter irons (cutters) which had been sharpened and were ready for use. The cutters were incised with the wedge & bar logo. The logo used on the "K" series planes does not include any caption below the words Keen Kutter. See illustration. The planes were made for Simmons by Stanley Rule and Level Company of New Britain, Connecticut.

Logo used on "K" Series Planes

Many of the catalog illustrations show the Keen Kutter logo and/or the words Keen Kutter on the sides of the planes. The actual hardware was not marked in this manner.

Each plane was packed in a separate cardboard box.

This section contains a listing, in numerical order, of all metal planes, wood bottom planes, routers and scrapers offered from 1913 through 1942.

"K" Bench Planes - Metal

The "K" series bench planes numbered K2 thru K8C are the family of flat bottom planes used for general purpose smoothing and fitting and for reducing stock size. K and the plane number are embossed forward of the front knob. The cutters are incised with the wedge & bar logo. The cutters and top irons of this series of planes are the thin untapered variety previously used by Stanley. The planes are finished with black enamel except for the sides and lever caps which are polished.

Each plane is fitted with lateral adjustment provisions. The lateral adjust lever is formed by a one half twist at the upper end. The front knobs are short. Nuts for securing the handles and knobs are made of brass. Most of the handles and knobs are made of rosewood. The planes numbered with a C have corrugated bottoms. The lengthwise corrugations are said to make the plane slide easier especially on resinous wood. The letter C does not appear on the part.

There are not any size 1 or 5 1/4 planes in this series.

K2 Smooth Plane $500 - $800
    Offered: 1913 thru 1929
    Length: 7 inches
    Width of Cutter: 1 5/8 inches

Type of Cutter: Double
Knob and Handle: Rosewood 1913 - 1920 & 1924 and later. Mahogany
    finish 1921- 1923
Lever Cap: Polished, no marking
Logo on the Cutter: Wedge & Bar
K2 embossed forward of the front knob
See K3 Smooth Plane illustration
The K2 is a general purpose smoothing plane small enough to use in
fitting trim and other very small workpieces. Many workmen found it too
small to fit the hand comfortably. This probably accounts for the reduced
sales and therefore the relative scarcity of this size plane

K2C Smooth Plane $800 - $1200
    Offered: 1913 thru 1920
    Same as the K2 except that this plane has a corrugated bottom instead of
    a smooth bottom
    See K3 Smooth Plane illustration

K3 Smooth Plane. Similar to K2, K2C,
K3C, K4, K4C, K4 1/2, K4 1/2C

K3 Smooth Plane $60 - $100
    Offered: 1913 thru 1941
    Length: 8 inches. 8 3/4 incheds observed not including the rear handle
        overhang Width of Cutter: 1 3/4 inches
    Type of Cutter: Double
    Knob and Handle: Rosewood 1913 - 1920 & 1924 - 1938, Mahogany
        finish 1921 - 1923, Walnut finish 1939 and later
    Lever Cap: Polished, no marking
    Logo on the Cutter: Wedge & Bar
    K3 embossed forward of the front knob
    The K3 is a general purpose smoothing plane appropriate for use on small
    workpieces in a cabinet or similar shop. This tool was also used in many
    tool kits where space was limited

K3C Smooth Plane $60 - $100
    Offered: 1913 thru 1941
    Same as the K3 except that this plane has a corrugated bottom instead of
        a smooth bottom
    See K3 Smooth Plane illustration

K4 Smooth Plane $45 - $75
    Offered: 1913 thru 1941
    Length: 9 inches
    Width of Cutter: 2 inches

Type of Cutter: Double
Knob and Handle: Rosewood 1913 - 1920 & 1924 - 1938, Mahogany
    finish 1921 - 1923, Walnut finish 1939 and later
Lever Cap: Polished, no marking
Logo on the Cutter: Wedge & Bar
K4 embossed forward of the front knob
See K3 Smooth Plane illustration
The K4 is a general purpose smoothing plane used for smoothing the face of a workpiece and for fitting small pieces. The throat is normally narrow and set for a fine shaving. The four is one of the most common sizes of Keen Kutter planes

K4C Smooth Plane $45 - $75
    Offered: 1913 thru 1941
    Same as the K4 except that this plane has a corrugated bottom instead of a smooth bottom
    See K3 Smooth Plane illustration

K4 1/2 Smooth Plane $75 - $145
    Offered: 1913 thru 1941
    Length: 10 inches
    Width of Cutter: 2 3/8 inches
    Type of Cutter: Double
    Knob and Handle: Rosewood 1913 - 1920 & 1924 - 1938, Mahogany
        finish 1921 - 1923, Walnut finish 1939 and later
    Lever Cap: Polished, no marking
    Logo on the Cutter: Wedge & Bar
    K4 1/2 embossed forward of the front knob
    See K3 Smooth Plane illustration
    The K4 1/2 is intended for use by a workman who prefers a slightly wider and heavier smooth plane

K4 1/2C Smooth Plane $75 - $145
    Offered: 1913 thru 1938
    Same as the K4 1/2 except that this plane has a corrugated bottom instead of a smooth bottom
    See K3 Smooth Plane illustration

K5 Jack Plane $45 - $75
    Offered: 1913 thru 1941
    Length: 14 inches
    Width of Cutter: 2 inches
    Type of Cutter: Double
    Knob and Handle: Rosewood 1913 - 1920 & 1924 - 1938, Mahogany
        finish 1921 - 1923, Walnut finish 1939 and later
    Lever Cap: Polished, no marking
    Logo on the Cutter: Wedge & Bar
    K5 embossed forward of the front knob
    See K6 Fore Plane illustration
    The Jack Plane is the workhorse of the plane family. It is a convenient middle size and is used for any and all bench plane functions
    The five is one of the most common sizes of Keen Kutter planes

K5C Smooth Plane $45 - $75
Offered: 1913 thru 1941
Same as the K5 except that this plane has a corrugated bottom instead of
a smooth bottom
See K6 Fore Plane illustration

K5 1/2 Jack Plane $60 - $80
Offered: 1913 thru 1941
Length: 15 inches
Width of Cutter: 2 1/4 inches 1913 thru 1938, 2 3/8 inches 1939 and later
Type of Cutter: Double
Knob and Handle: Rosewood 1913 - 1920 & 1924 - 1938, Mahogany finish
    1921 - 1923, Walnut finish 1939 and later
Lever Cap: Polished, no marking
Logo on the Cutter: Wedge & Bar
K5 1/2 embossed forward of the front knob
See K6 Fore Plane illustration
The K5 1/2 is intended for use by a workman who prefers a slightly wider
and heavier jack plane.

K5 1/2C Jack Plane $60 - $80
Offered: 1913 thru 1941
Same as the K5 1/2 except that this plane has a corrugated bottom instead
of a smooth bottom
See K6 Fore Plane illustration

K6 Fore Plane. Similar to K5, K5C,
K5 1/2, K5 1/2C, K6C, K7, K7C, K8, K8C

K6 Fore Plane $45 - $75
Offered: 1913 thru 1941
Length: 18 inches
Width of Cutter: 2 3/8 inches
Type of Cutter: Double
Knob and Handle: Rosewood 1913 - 1920 & 1924 - 1938, Mahogany
    finish 1921 - 1923, Walnut finish 1939 and later
Lever Cap: Polished, no marking
Logo on the Cutter: Wedge & Bar
K6 embossed forward of the front knob

The K6 Fore Plane is actually a short jointer. It is sometimes used before the jointer plane allowing the jointer to be kept extra sharp to make the final cut for edge joining

K6C Fore Plane $45 - $75
    Offered: 1913 thru 1941
    Same as the K6 except that this plane has a corrugated bottom instead of a smooth bottom
    See K6 Fore Plane illustration

K7 Jointer Plane $55 - $90
    Offered: 1913 thru 1938
    Length: 22 inches
    Width of Cutter: 2 3/8 inches
    Type of Cutter: Double
    Knob and Handle: Rosewood 1913 - 1920 & 1924 and later, Mahogany finish 1921 - 1923
    Lever Cap: Polished, no marking
    Logo on the Cutter: Wedge & Bar
    K7 embossed forward of the front knob
    See K6 Fore Plane illustration
    The K7 is used primarily for edge joining long boards and for final trimming of long workpieces such as doors

K7C Jointer Plane $55 - $90
    Offered: 1913 thru 1934
    Same as the K7 except that this plane has a corrugated bottom instead of a smooth bottom
    See K6 Fore Plane illustration

K8 Jointer Plane $75 - $110
    Offered: 1913 thru 1938
    Length: 24 inches
    Width of Cutter: 2 5/8 inches
    Type of Cutter: Double
    Knob and Handle: Rosewood 1913 - 1920 & 1924 and later, Mahogany finish 1921 - 1923
    Lever Cap: Polished, no marking
    Logo on the Cutter: Wedge & Bar
    K8 embossed forward of the front knob
    See K6 Fore Plane illustration
    The K8 is the longest of the metal planes in this series and is used where maximum accuracy is desired. Its extra length and weight reduces waviness of the cut to a minimum

K8C Jointer Plane $75 - $110
    Offered: 1913 thru 1938
    Same as the K8 except that this plane has a corrugated bottom instead of a smooth bottom
    See K6 Fore Plane illustration

K9 1/2 Block Plane. Similar to K15, K16, K17

K9 1/2 Block Plane $45 - $60
  Offered: 1913 thru 1942
  Length: 6 inches. 6 1/4 inches observed
  Width of Cutter: 1 5/8 inches
  Logo on the Cutter: Wedge & Bar
  K9 1/2 incised on the lateral adjust lever. The casting is not marked
  Screw and lateral adjustment of the cutter and throat adjustment provisions
  The K9 1/2 is a popular block plane that is fully adjustable. It is used primarily for end trimming (blocking in) of the workpiece

K9 3/4 Block Plane

K9 3/4 Block Plane $375 - $450
  Offered: 1913 thru 1929
  Length: 6 inches. 6 1/4 inches observed
  Width of Cutter: 1 5/8 inches
  Handle: Rosewood 1913 - 1920, Mahogany finish 1921 - 1923, Rosewood finish 1924 and later
  Logo on the Cutter: Wedge & Bar
  K9 3/4 incised on the lateral adjust lever
  The casting is not marked
  Screw and lateral adjustment of the cutter and throat adjustment provisions

The K9 3/4 is the same as the K9 1/2 except for the rear handle. The handle and handle attachment were often damaged during use. Beware of repaired or replaced parts

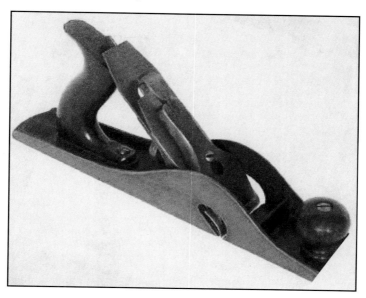

K10 Carriage Maker's Rabbet Plane

K10 Carriage Makers' Jointer Plane $175 - $250
    Offered: 1913 thru 1920
    Length: 13 inches
    Width of Cutter: 2 1/8 inches
    Type of Cutter: Double
    Knob and Handle: Rosewood
    Lever Cap: Polished, no marking
    Logo on the Cutter: Wedge & Bar
    K10 embossed forward of the knob
    Has screw and lateral adjustment of the cutter. The lateral adjust lever was formed by a one-half twist at the upper end
    The K10 is used to cut a rabbet in a long workpiece where minimum waviness is required. It was also recommended for heavy tasks such as bridge or mill work

K10 1/2 Carriage Makers' Jointer Plane $200 - $350
    Offered: 1913 thru 1923
    Length: 9 inches
    Width of Cutter: 2 1/8 inches
    Type of Cutter: Double
    Knob and Handle: Rosewood

K10 1/2 Carriage Maker's Rabbet Plane

Lever Cap: Polished, no marking
Logo on the Cutter: Wedge & Bar
K10 1/2 embossed behind the frog
Has screw and lateral adjustment of the cutter. The lateral adjust lever was formed by a one-half twist at the upper end
The K10 1/2 is a convenient middle sized rabbet and is somewhat easier to use than the shorter rabbet planes

K15 Block Plane $40 - $60
    Offered: 1913 thru 1941
    Length: 7 inches
    Width of Cutter: 1 5/8 inches
    Logo on the Cutter: Wedge & Bar
    K15 incised on the lateral adjust lever. The casting is not marked
    See K9 1/2 Block Plane illustration
    The K15 is the same as the K9 1/2 except for length

K16 Block Plane $40 - $65
    Offered: 1914 thru 1929
    Length: 6 inches
    Width of Cutter: 1 5/8 inches
    Finish: Nickel plated trimmings
    Logo on the Cutter: Wedge & Bar
    K16 incised on the lateral adjust lever. The casting is not marked
    See K9 1/2 Block Plane illustration
    The K16 is the same as the K9 1/2 except for finish

K17 Block Plane $40 - $65
    Offered: 1914 thru 1920
    Length: 7 inches
    Width of Cutter: 1 5/8 inches
    Finish: Nickel plated trimmings
    Logo on the Cutter: Wedge & Bar
    K17 incised on the lateral adjust lever. The casting is not marked
    See K9 1/2 Block Plane illustration
    The K17 is the same as the K15 except for finish

K18 Block Plane, Knuckle Joint. Similar to K19

K18 Block Plane, Knuckle Joint $50 - $80
  Offered: 1913 thru 1941
  Length: 6 inches, 1913 thru 1938, 6 1/4 inches,1939 and later
  Width of Cutter: 1 5/8 inches
  Finish: Nickel plated trimmings
  Logo on the Cutter: Wedge & Bar
  Keen Kutter incised on the lever cap
  K18 incised on the lateral adjust lever. The casting is not marked
  Has screw and lateral adjustment of the cutter and throat adjustment
  provisions
  The K18 has the same features as the K9 1/2 Block Plane except for the
  knuckle joint lever cap
  Later K18 planes have improved lever caps per the 2-18-13 Bodmer &
  Burdick patent. See lever cap illustration. It is assumed that the patent
  date was deleted from the cap at some later date resulting in a third vari-
  ety of K18 plane

K19 Block Plane, Knuckle Joint $55 - $90
  Offered: 1913 thru 1929
  Length: 7 inches
  Keen Kutter incised on the lever cap
  K19 incised on the lateral adjust lever. The casting is not marked
  See K18 Block Plane, Knuckle Joint illustration
  The K19 is the same as the K18 except for length

"K" Bench Planes - Wood Bottom

The "K" series of wood bottom bench planes, numbered K22 thru K36, are the family
of flat bottom planes used for general purpose smoothing and fitting and for reducing stock
size. The K number and the logo are incised on the forward end of the plane. The double
cutters are incised with the wedge and bar logo. The cutters and top irons of this series of
planes are the thin untapered variety previously used by Stanley. The metal portions of the
planes are finished with black enamel. The catalog descriptive material states that the lever
caps are polished; however, the caps noted on this series of planes are painted black.

Each plane is fitted with lateral adjustment provisions. The lateral adjust lever is formed
by a one half twist at the upper end. Knobs, handles, and bottoms are made of beechwood.
Hold-down bolts for the front knobs are made of steel. Brass screwdriver nuts are used for
the rear handles. The catalog picture markings shown on the sides of the wood bottoms do
not appear on the actual planes.

The wood bottoms of these planes are quite subject to wear and cracking. In many
cases the bottoms have been dressed down by the user to maintain squareness or by a tool
dealer for the sake of appearance. In some cases the longer varieties have been cut off so
that they will fit into a chicken box. Any modification or excessive deterioration greatly
reduces value.

There are not any size 25 planes in this series.

K22 Smooth Plane, Wood Bottom $40 - $65

K22 Smooth Plane, wood bottom. Similar to K23, K24

Offered: 1914 thru 1920
Length: 8 inches
Width of Cutter: 1 3/4 inches
Type of Cutter: Double
Wood Parts: Beechwood
Lever Cap: No marking
Logo on the Cutter: Wedge & Bar
K22 and logo incised on the toe

K23 Smooth Plane, Wood Bottom $40 - $65
Offered: 1913 thru 1920
Length: 9 inches
Width of Cutter: 1 3/4 inches
Type of Cutter: Double
Wood Parts: Beechwood
Lever Cap: No marking
Logo on the Cutter: Wedge & Bar
K23 and logo incised on the toe
See K22 Smooth Plane illustration
The K23 is the same as the K22 except for size

K24 Smooth Plane, Wood Bottom $35 - $60
Offered: 1913 thru 1938
Length: 8 inches. 9 inches observed
Width of Cutter: 2 inches
Type of Cutter: Double
Wood Parts: Beechwood
Lever Cap: No marking
Logo on the Cutter: Wedge & Bar
K24 and logo incised on the toe
See K22 Smooth Plane illustration
The K24 is the same as the K22 except for size

K26 Jack Plane, wood bottom.
Similar to K27, K27 1/2, K28, K29,
K30, K31, K32, K33, K34

K26 Jack Plane, Wood Bottom $35 - $60
Offered: 1913 thru 1938
Length: 15 inches
Width of Cutter: 2 inches
Type of Cutter: Double
Wood Parts: Beechwood

Lever Cap: No marking
Logo on the Cutter: Wedge & Bar
K26 and logo incised on the toe

K27 Jack Plane, Wood Bottom $40 - $65
Offered: 1913 thru 1920
Length: 15 inches
Width of Cutter: 2 1/8 inches
Type of Cutter: Double
Wood Parts: Beechwood
Lever Cap: No marking
Logo on the Cutter: Wedge & Bar
K27 and logo incised on the toe
See K26 Jack Plane illustration
The K27 is the same as the K26 except for size

K27 1/2 Jack Plane, Wood Bottom $45 - $75
Offered: 1914 thru 1920
Length: 15 inches
Width of Cutter: 2 1/4 inches
Type of Cutter: Double
Wood Parts: Beechwood
Lever Cap: No marking
Logo on the Cutter: Wedge & Bar
K27 1/2 and logo incised on the toe
See K26 Jack Plane illustration
The K27 1/2 is the same as the K26 except for size

K28 Fore Plane, Wood Bottom $35 - $60
Offered: 1913 thru 1934
Length: 18 inches
Width of Cutter: 2 3/8 inches
Type of Cutter: Double
Wood Parts: Beechwood
Lever Cap: No marking
Logo on the Cutter: Wedge & Bar
K28 and logo incised on the toe
See K26 Jack Plane illustration
The K28 is the same as the K26 except for size

K29 Fore Plane, Wood Bottom $40 - $65
Offered: 1913 thru 1920
Length: 20 inches
Width of Cutter: 2 3/8 inches
Type of Cutter: Double
Wood Parts: Beechwood
Lever Cap: No marking
Logo on the Cutter: Wedge & Bar
K29 and logo incised on the toe
See K26 Jack Plane illustration
The K29 is the same as the K26 except for size

K30 Jointer Plane, Wood Bottom $40 - $65
    Offered: 1913 thru 1920
    Length: 22 inches
    Width of Cutter: 2 3/8 inches
    Type of Cutter: Double
    Wood Parts: Beechwood
    Lever Cap: No marking
    Logo on the Cutter: Wedge & Bar
    K30 and logo incised on the toe
    See K26 Jack Plane illustration
    The K30 is the same as the K26 except for size

K31 Jointer Plane, Wood Bottom $35 - $65
    Offered: 1913 thru 1929
    Length: 24 inches
    Width of Cutter: 2 3/8 inches
    Type of Cutter: Double
    Wood Parts: Beechwood
    Lever Cap: No marking
    Logo on the Cutter: Wedge & Bar
    K31 and logo incised on the toe
    See K26 Jack Plane illustration
    The K31 is the same as the K26 except for size

K32 Jointer Plane, Wood Bottom $35 - $65
    Offered: 1913 thru 1929
    Length: 26 inches
    Width of Cutter: 2 5/8 inches
    Type of Cutter: Double
    Wood Parts: Beechwood
    Lever Cap: No marking
    Logo on the Cutter: Wedge & Bar
    K32 and logo incised on the toe
    See K26 Jack Plane illustration
    The K32 is the same as the K26 except for size

K33 Jointer Plane, Wood Bottom $40 - $70
    Offered: 1913 thru 1920
    Length: 28 inches
    Width of Cutter: 2 5/8 inches
    Type of Cutter: Double
    Wood Parts: Beechwood
    Lever Cap: No marking
    Logo on the Cutter: Wedge & Bar
    K33 and logo incised on the toe
    See K26 Jack Plane illustration
    The K33 is the same as the K26 except for size

K34 Jointer Plane, Wood Bottom $40 - $70
    Offered: 1914 thru 1920
    Length: 30 inches
    Width of Cutter: 2 5/8 inches

Type of Cutter: Double
Wood Parts: Beechwood
Lever Cap: No marking
Logo on the Cutter: Wedge & Bar
K34 and logo incised on the toe
See K26 Jack Plane illustration
The K34 is the same as the K26 except for size

K35 Smooth Plane, handled, wood bottom. Similar to K36

K35 Smooth Plane, Handled, Wood Bottom $40 - $65
    Offered: 1913 thru 1938
    Length: 9 inches. 8 5/8 inches observed
    Width of Cutter: 2 inches
    Type of Cutter: Double
    Wood Parts: Beechwood
    Lever Cap: No marking
    Logo on the Cutter: Wedge & Bar
    K35 and logo incised on the toe

K36 Smooth Plane, Handled, Wood Bottom $40 - $65
    Offered: 1913 thru 1938
    Length: 10 inches
    Width of Cutter: 2 3/8 inches
    Type of Cutter: Double
    Wood Parts: Beechwood
    Lever Cap: No marking
    Logo on the Cutter: Wedge & Bar
    K36 and logo incised on the toe
    See K35 Smooth Plane, Handled illustration
    The K36 is the same as the K35 except for size

K60 Block Plane, low angle. Similar to K65 (pp. 87-88)

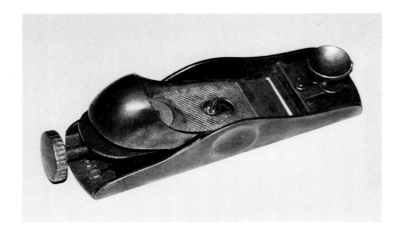

K60 Block Plane, Low Angle $45 - $60
    Offered: 1913 thru 1942
    Length: 6 inches
    Width of Cutter: 1 3/8 inches
    Finish: Nickel plated trimmings 1918 and later per catalogs
    Logo on the Cutter: Wedge & Bar
    Keen Kutter incised on the lever cap
    K60 embossed on the rear of the casting
    Has screw adjustment of the cutter and throat adjustment provisions
    It is probable that all K60 planes have nickel plated trimmings

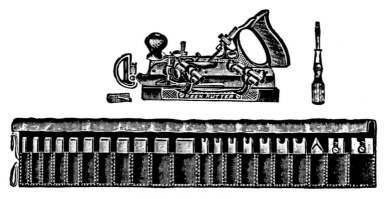

K64 Combination Plane

K64 Combination Plane $800 - $1400
    Offered: 1914 thru 1934
    Length: 11 inches overall
    Width of Cutters; 21 provided. Seven beading - 1/8, 3/16, 5/16, 1/4, 3/8,
        7/16, 1/2 inches.; ten plow and dado - 1/8, 3/16, 1/4, 5/16, 3/8, 7/16,
        1/2, 5/8, 3/4, 7/8 inches; one sash tool, one match tool, one filletster,
        and one slitting tool

Finish: Nickel plated
Handle and Knob: Rosewood
Logo on the Cutters: Wedge & Bar. The narrow cutters are marked Keen
  Kutter outside of the logo
K64 is embossed on the right side of the main stock and on the center
sliding section. Keen Kutter is embossed on the metal portion of the fence
A cam rest, a K50/2 screw driver and both short and long arms are pro-
vided. The cam rest is marked Keen Kutter
The cutters are put up in a red flannel roll 1914 thru 1917 and in a brown
canvas roll 1918 and later. Other types of material have been observed
The K64 is a combination beading, rabbet and slitting plane
The short depth stop shown in the catalog illustrations is not mentioned in
the descriptions and is not shown in the parts list. Planes have been observed with and without these stops. It is considered probable that the set
of parts delivered with the plane did not include this item
Beware of replaced parts, especially unmarked cutters and cam rest

K65 Block Plane, Low Angle $45 - $65
    Offered: 1913 thru 1934
    Length: 7 inches
    Width of Cutter: 1 5/8 inches
    Finish: Nickel plated trimmings 1918 and later per catalogs
    Logo on the Cutter: Wedge & Bar
    Keen Kutter incised on the lever cap
    K65 embossed on the rear of the casting
    See K60 Block Plane, Low Angle illustration
    The K65 is the same as K60 Block Plane except for size
    It is probable that all K65 planes have nickel plated trimmings

K75 Rabbet Plane, bull nose

K75 Rabbet Plane, Bull Nose $125 - $175
    Offered: 1913 thru 1934
    Length: 4 inches
    Width of Cutter: 1 inch
    Logo on the Cutter: Wedge & Bar
    K75 embossed aft of the cutter
    Not adjustable.

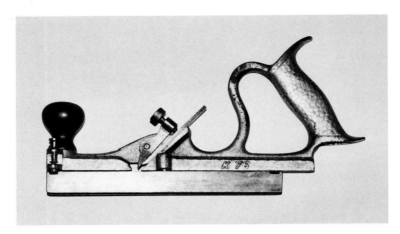

K76 Tonguing and Grooving Plane

K76 Tonguing and Grooving Plane $150 - $210
 Offered: 1914 thru 1929
 Length: 9 inches (Sole)
 Knob: Rosewood
 Finish: Nickel plated
 Logo on the Cutters: Wedge & Bar
 K76 embossed on the left side of the casting
 The fence pivots in the center which allows the plane to cut either a tongue or a matching groove.
 For use on 3/4 to 1 1/4 inch stock. Centers on 7/8 inch stock. Cuts a 5/16 inch groove
 Provided with three cutters. One cutter is extra wide to allow use of the plane on thick stock. Beware of replaced or missing cutters

K78 Rabbet and
Filletster Plane

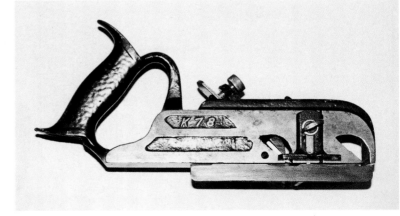

K78 Rabbet and Filletster Plane $100 - $175
     Offered: 1914 thru 1934
     Length: 8 1/2 inches (Sole)
     Width of Cutter: 1 1/2 inches
     Logo on the Cutters: Wedge & Bar
     K78 embossed on the right side of the casting
     Has a right hand spur and depth stop.
     Two cutter seats allow the plane to be used for either regular or bull nose
         work
     The casting is machined flat on both sides
     An adjustable fence is provided.

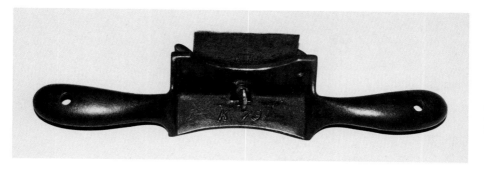

K79 Cabinet Scraper

K79 Cabinet Scraper $45 - $60
     Offered: 1913 thru 1938
     Length: 11 1/4 inches
     Width of Blade: 2 3/4 inches
     Finish: Nickel plated 1913 thru 1920
     Logo on the Blade: Wedge & Bar
     The logo is also incised on the blade retaining bar
     K79 embossed on the casting

K90 Cabinet Scraper

K90 Cabinet Scraper $35 - $55
    Offered: 1912 thru 1938
    Length: 11 inches
    Width of Blade: 3 inches. 2 7/8 inches observed
    Finish: Blade holder is unfinished
    Handle: Hardwood painted black
    Logo on the Blade Holder: Wedge & Bar
    Has a ball and socket tilt adjustment
    The blade is not marked
    Patented August 9, 1910

K102 Block Plane

K102 Block Plane $25 - $40
    Offered: 1913 thru 1942
    Length: 5 1/2 inches
    Width of Cutter: 1 1/4 inches
    Logo on the Cutter: Wedge & Bar
    K102 embossed aft of the finger rest
    Not adjustable

K103 Block Plane

K103 Block Plane $25 - $40
    Offered: 1913 thru 1942
    Length: 5 1/2 inches
    Width of Cutter: 1 1/4 inches. 1 5/16 and 1 3/8 inches observed
    Logo on the Cutter: Wedge & Bar
    K103 embossed aft of the finger rest
    Lever adjustment of the cutter
    The K103 is one of the most common of Keen Kutter planes

K110 Block Plane

K110 Block Plane $25 - $40
    Offered: 1913 thru 1942
    Length: 7 1/2 inches. 7 1/8 inches observed
    Width of Cutter: 1 5/8 inches
    Knob: Fruitwood or stained hardwood
    Logo on the Cutter: Wedge & Bar
    K110 embossed forward of the knob
    Not adjustable
    The K110 is one of the most common of Keen Kutter planes

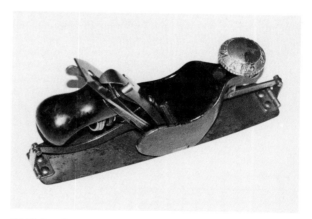

K115 Circular Plane

K115 Circular Plane $250 - $400
    Offered: 1913 thru 1929
    Length: 10 inches. 10 1/4 inches observed
    Width of Cutter: 1 3/4 inches
    Logo on the Cutter: Wedge & Bar
    K115 embossed on the adjustment knob
    The casting is not marked
    Screw and lateral adjustment of the cutter. The lateral adjust lever was formed
    by a one-half twist at the upper end
    The flexible steel sole allows the plane to be used on either a concave or a
    convex surface

K120 Block Plane

K120 Block Plane $25 - $40
    Offered: 1913 thru 1940
    Length: 7 1/2 inches. 7 1/8 inches observed
    Width of Cutter: 1 5/8 inches
    Knob: Fruitwood or stained hardwood
    Logo on the Cutter: Wedge & Bar
    K120 embossed forward of the knob
    Lever adjustment of the cutter

K130 Block Plane, Double Ender

K130 Block Plane, Double Ender $85 - $120
    Offered: 1913 thru 1934
    Length: 8 inches
    Width of Cutter: 1 5/8 inches
    Knob: Rosewood 1913 - 1923, hardwood 1924 and later
    Logo on the Cutter: Wedge & Bar
    K130 embossed forward of the knob
    Not adjustable
    The two cutter seats allow the plane to be used for regular or bull nose work

K140 Rabbet and Block Plane

K140 Rabbet and Block Plane $175 - $275
    Offered: 1913 thru 1929
    Length: 7 inches
    Width of Cutter: 1 3/4 inches
    Knob: Rosewood 1913 thru 1923, hardwood 1924 and later
    Finish: Nickel plated trimmings 1918 and later per catalog
    Logo on the Cutter: Wedge & Bar
    K140 embossed forward of the knob
    Screw adjustment of the cutter
    This plane has a removable side plate that allows the plane to be used as
    either a rabbet or a block plane. The Keen Kutter logo is incised on the
    removable side.
    It is probable that all K140 planes have nickel plated trimmings

K171 Router, Open Throat

K171 Router, Open Throat $110 - $160
Offered: 1913 thru 1938
Length: 7 1/2 inches
Width of Cutters: Two provided - 1/4 and 1/2 inch
Knob: Rosewood. Hardwood observed
Finish: Nickel plated
K171 embossed on the casting
Has a throat closing attachment. Hold-down screws for the knobs are made of steel
The two holes appear to be for attachment of a fence. However, the catalog descriptions do not mention a fence
A thumb wheel is provided for adjustment of the cutter. The cutters are notched to mate with the wheel
This tool is unique in that it has a Keen Kutter logo incised two places on the bottom surface

K171 1/2 Router, closed throat

K171 1/2 Router, Closed Throat $110 - $160
Offered: 1913 thru 1923
Length: 7 5/8 inches
Width of Cutters: Two provided - 1/4 and 1/2 inch
Knobs: Rosewood
Finish: Nickel plated
K171 1/2 embossed on the casting
Hold-down screws for the knobs are made of steel.
The two holes appear to be for attachment of a fence. However, the catalog descriptions do not mention a fence
A thumb wheel is provided for adjustment of the cutter. The cutters are notched to mate with the wheel.
This tool is unique in that it has a Keen Kutter logo incised two places on the bottom surface

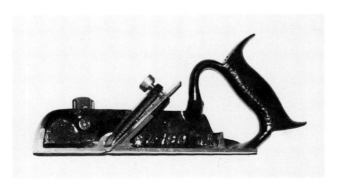

96

K190 Rabbet Plane. Similar to K191, K192 (pp.96-97)

K190 Rabbet Plane $175 - $225
   Offered: 1913 thru 1929
   Length: 8 inches (sole). 8 1/4 inches observed
   Width of Cutter: 1 1/2 inches
   Logo on the Cutter: Wedge & Bar
   K190 embossed on the left side of the casting
   Has a right hand spur and depth stop
   Both sides of the casting are machined flat

K191 Rabbet Plane $175 - $225
   Offered: 1913 thru 1929
   Length: 8 inches (sole)
   Width of Cutter: 1 1/4 inches
   Logo on the Cutter: Wedge & Bar
   K191 embossed on the left side of the casting
   See K190 Rabbet Plane illustration
   Same as the K190 Rabbet Plane except for width

K192 Rabbet Plane $175 - $225
   Offered: 1913 thru 1923
   Length: 8 inches (sole)
   Width of Cutter: 1 inch
   Logo on the Cutter: Wedge & Bar
   K192 embossed on the left side of the casting
   See K190 Rabbet Plane illustration.
   Same as the K190 Rabbet Plane except for width

K200 Circular Plane

K200 Circular Plane $800 - $1200
   Offered: 1914 thru 1920
   Length: 10 inches
   Width of Cutter: 1 3/4 inches
   Finish: Black enamel. Late models are nickel plated

Logo on the Cutter: Wedge & Bar
Logo is embossed on the forward end of the casting
Keen Kutter K200 embossed on the adjustment knob
Has screw and lateral adjustment of the cutter
The lateral adjust lever was formed by a one-half twist at the upper end
The flexible steel sole allows the plane to be used on a either a concave or a convex surface

K212 Veneer or Cabinet Scraper

K212 Veneer or Cabinet Scraper $175 - $250
    Offered: 1913 thru 1923
    Length: 6 1/4 inches. 6 3/8 inches observed
    Width of Blade: 3 inches. 2 15/16 inches observed
    Handle: Rosewood
    Logo on the Blade: Wedge & Bar
    K212 embossed forward of the blade
    Blade angle is adjustable

K220 Block Plane

K220 Block Plane $25 - $45
    Offered: 1913 thru 1942
    Length: 7 1/2 inches. 7 1/8 inches observed
    Width of Cutter: 1 5/8 inches
    Knob: Rosewood 1913 - 1923, hardwood 1924 and later
    Logo on the Cutter: Wedge & Bar
    K220 embossed forward of the knob
    Has screw adjustment of the cutter

K240 Scrub Plane

K240 Scrub Plane $120 - $175
    Offered: 1913 thru 1929
    Length: 9 1/2 inches. 9 3/4 inches observed
    Width of Cutter: 1 1/4 inches
    Type of Cutter: Single
    Knob and Handle: Beechwood, natural finish

Logo on the Cutter: Wedge & Bar
K240 embossed forward of the knob
Not adjustable
Lever cap and sides of the plane are painted black as well as the inside of
the base
The plane is intended to be used for roughing down work before the use of
the smoothing or jack plane. The cutter has a rounded cutting edge

K312 Scraper

K312 Scraper $250 - $350
    Offered: 1913 thru 1920
    Length: 9 inches
    Width of Blade: 3 inches
    Knob and Handle: Rosewood
    Logo on the Cutter: Wedge & Bar
    K312 embossed aft of the knob
    Blade angle is adjustable

Cabinet Scraper

Cabinet Scraper $25 - $40
    Offered: 1912 thru 1941
    Size: K24 2 x 4 inches 1912 thru 1934, K255 2 1/2 x 5 inches, K33 3 x 3
        inches 1913 thru 1934, K35 3 x 5 inches, K356 3 1/2 x 6 inches, K46
        4 x 6 inches 1912 thru 1938
    Logo: Wedge & Bar, Cutlery and Tools
    These are flat steel scrapers without handles. Polished and tempered
    Neither the catalog number nor the size is shown on the hardware

Keen Kutter Planes by Shapleigh

Remaining Simmons Stock

Shapleigh Hardware Company bought Simmons in mid 1940 including the Keen Kutter trademarks. The first catalog update (late 1940), after the Shapleigh purchase, included some Keen Kutter "K" series bench planes and few block planes. The 1942 catalog listed the block planes only. The illustrations in both of these catalogs are poor and in some cases incomplete. However, it appears that the intent was too close out the remaining stock of K series planes. The Simmons agreement to purchase planes from Stanley was probably terminated when Simmons was sold to Shapleigh. It is also known that Stanley drastically reduced production of consumer goods in the early 1940s because of the war effort. In any case, it is fairly certain that production of Keen Kutter planes was halted until after World War II.

Post World War II Planes

Post World War II KK planes - Stanley

Metal bench planes have been noted with the words Keen Kutter embossed on the lever cap. The words are enclosed within a rectangle with a red background. See illustration. These planes are numbered with a simple numerical digit (i.e. No 5) rather than with a K. Several block planes assumed to be of this vintage have also been noted. The block planes are not marked on the castings. The E. C. Simmons Keen Kutter logo is incised on the cutters of both the bench and the block planes. The detail characteristics of this series of planes are similar to Stanley post-World War II production. These planes are quite scarce and command a slightly higher price than the later Shapleigh KK planes of similar size.

Another variety of jack plane having the words Keen Kutter deeply incised on the lever cap has been noted. In this case the words are painted red and are not enclosed within a rectangle. See illustration. The casting on this plane is not marked. The casting and frog are painted a red-orange color. The E. C. Simmons Keen Kutter logo is incised on the cutter The detail characteristics match those of Millers Falls Company planes of the period.

Dating of any of the above planes has not been firmly established. However, it can be reasonably concluded that they were distributed by Shapleigh Hardware Company at some point from 1948 thru 1949 inclusive.

Late Shapleigh Keen Kutter Planes

Several bench planes with the Keen Kutter wedge and bar logo on the lever cap are shown in the Shapleigh catalogs of the early 1950s and later. The earliest available reference to a plane in this series in dated 1950. The lever cap logo on these planes have the words Keen Kutter only and have a red background. The lever caps and brass adjusting nuts are nickel plated. The knobs and handles are made of hardwood with a mahogany finish. The knobs are tall. The double cutters are incised with the wedge and bar logo. The words E. C. Simmons are included within the outline of the cutter logo on the early variety of planes of this type. The base castings are painted black. The frogs are painted black on early planes and red on later models.

The plane numbers are for ordering and stocking purposes and do not appear on the hardware. This series of planes was made for Shapleigh by Sargent and Company.

The following planes were listed:

KKM3 Smooth Plane $60 - $90
 Offered: 1950 thru 1958
 Length: 8 inches
 Width of Cutter: 1 3/4 inches
 See KKM4 illustration

KKM4 Smooth Plane $40 - $65
 Offered: 1950 and later
 Length: 10 inches 1950 thru
  1956, 9 inches 1957 and
  later
 Width of Cutter: 2 inches

KKM4 Smooth Plane. Similar to KKM3

KKM5 Jack Plane. Similar to K5C, KC6, KC7

KKM5 Jack Plane $50 thru $75
    Offered: 1950 and later
    Length: 14 inches
    Width of Cutter: 2 inches

KC5 Jack Plane, Corrugated $60 - $85
    Offered: 1950 thru 1956
    Length: 14 inches
    Width of Cutter: 2 inches
    See KKM5 Jack Plane illustration

KC6 Fore Plane, Corrugated $60 - $85
    Offered: 1950 thru 1956
    Length: 18 inches
    Width of Cutter: 2 3/8 inches
    See KKM5 Jack Plane illustration

KC7 Jointer Plane, Corrugated $70 - $100
    Offered: 1950 thru 1956
    Length: 22 inches
    Width of Cutter: 2 3/8 inches
    See KKM5 Jack Plane illustration

Four types of Keen Kutter block planes and one rabbet and filletster plane were listed in the late Shapleigh catalogs. The cutters in these planes are incised with the wedge and bar logo with only the words Keen Kutter within the logo outline. The castings are not marked. The planes were made for Shapleigh by Sargent and Company.

KKM9 1/2 Block Plane $40 - $60
    Offered: 1950 and later
    Length: 6 inches
    Width of Cutter: 1 5/8 inches
    Finish: Nickel plated trimmings
    Has screw and lateral adjustment of the cutter and throat adjustment provisions

KKM9 1/2 Block Plane

KKM60 Block Plane, Low Angle $40 - $60
  Offered: 1959 only
  Length: 6 inches
  Width of Cutter: 1 3/8 inches

KKM110 Block Plane $30 - $50

KKM110 Block Plane

  Offered: 1950 thru 1958
  Length: 7 inches. 7 1/16 and 7 3/16 inches observed
  Width of Cutter: 1 5/8 inches
  Finish: Nickel plated cap. Japanned cap observed
  Knob: Stained hardwood
  Not adjustable

KM78 Rabbet and Filletster Plane

KM78 Rabbet and Filletster Plane $100 - $175
  Offered: 1950 thru 1957
  Length: 8 1/2 inches. 8 3/16 inches observed
  Width of Cutter: 1 1/2 inches

An adjustable fence, right hand spur and depth stop are provided
Two cutter seats allow the plane to be used for either regular or bull nose work
The casting is machined flat on both sides

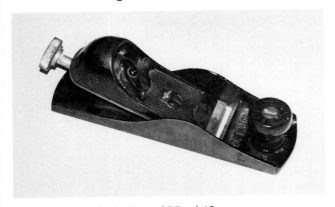

KKM220 Block Plane

KKM220 Block Plane $25 - $40
    Offered: 1950 thru 1958
    Length: 7 inches. 7 1/8 inches observed
    Width of Cutter: 1 5/8 inches
    Finish: Nickel plated cap. Japanned cap also observed
    Knob: Stained hardwood
    Has screw adjustment of the cutter

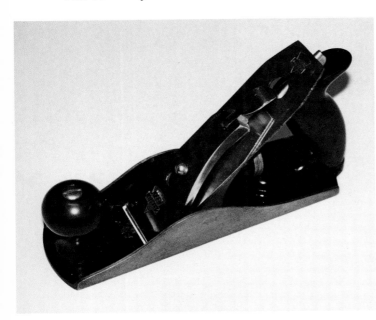

Latest KK Bench Plane

Latest Variety of Keen Kutter Smooth Plane $40 - $65

An unused Keen Kutter smooth plane has been observed that is similar to the KKM4 plane except that it has a black plastic handle and knob. It has a black base and a red frog as seen on other late model Keen Kutter planes. The label on the original Shapleigh Hardware Company box includes the number F3929GK rather than the KKM4 designation. This plane is not shown in any available catalog. It is assumed to be the latest variety of Keen Kutter plane.

Simmons Planes

Simmons Hardware Company offered a line of low priced promotional tools called Simmons Leader starting in 1935. The planes in this series are marked Simmons; the word Leader does not appear on the hardware. Marking is on the cutter only and does not include a size or number designation. The frogs of the bench planes were generally made of bent-up steel rather than being cast. However, one plane has been noted having the frog cast as part of the base.

Catalog illustrations show tall knobs on the bench planes; however, most of the planes noted have short knobs. None of the lever caps on Simmons bench planes show any evidence of being painted as stated in the catalog descriptions.

The following planes were listed:

SV1 Block Plane

SV1 Block Plane $25 - $35
    Offered: 1935 thru 1940
    Length: 7 1/4 inches
    Width of Cutter: 1 5/8 inches
    Knob: Hardwood stained mahogany
    Marking on Cutter: Simmons
    Not adjustable.

SV2 Smooth Plane $25 - $35
    Offered: 1935 thru 1940
    Length: 8 inches. 9 1/4 inches
      observed
    Width of Cutter: 1 3/4 inches
    Knob and Handle: Hardwood
      with rosewood stain
    Finish: Japanned casting per
      catalog
    Marking on the Cutter:
      Simmons
    Has screw and lateral adjustment of the cutter. The lateral adjust lever has the upper end bent down on both sides
    Some of planes observed have the casting painted a dull red color and the frog painted blue
    The catalog descriptions state that the lever caps are cast. A bent-up sheet metal cap has also been observed

SV2 Smooth Plane. Similar to SV3

SV3 Smooth Plane $25 - $35
    Offered: 1935 thru 1940
    Length: 9 inches. 10 inches observed
    Width of Cutter: 2 inches
    Knob and Handle: Hardwood with rosewood stain
    Finish: Japanned casting per catalog
    Marking on the Cutter: Simmons
    See SV2 Smooth Plane illustration
    Same as the SV2 except for size

SV4 Jack Plane

SV4 Jack Plane $25 - $35
    Offered: 1935 thru 1940
    Length: 14 inches. 13 1/2 inches observed
    Width of Cutter: 2 inches
    Knob and Handle: Hardwood with rosewood stain
    Finish: Japanned casting per catalog
    Marking on the Cutter: Simmons
    Has screw and lateral adjustment of the cutter. The lateral adjust lever
    has the upper end bent down on both sides
    Some of planes observed have the casting painted a dull red color and
    the frog painted blue

S/2 Cabinet Scraper $20 - $25
    Offered: 1935 thru 1941
    Length: 12 1/2 inches
    Width of Blade: 3 inches
    Handle: Beechwood
    Marking on the Blade: Simmons

S/2 Cabinet Scraper

Cabinet Scraper $15 - $25
    Offered: 1935 through 1938
    Size: S/24 2 x 4 inches, S/255 2 1/2 x 5 inches,
    S/35 3 x 5 inches, S/356 3 1/2 x 6 inches
    Marking: Simmons
    Polished and tempered
    These are flat steel scrapers without handles

Cabinet Scraper

Chip-A-Way Planes

Chip-A-Way Wooden Planes $20 - $35 Each

A early variety of Chip-A-Way wooden bench planes was offered by Simmons Hardware Company from 1904 thru 1906. Chip-A-Way was listed as a registered trademark and the name was used on a number of second quality tools including these planes. The planes are similar to the Keen Kutter planes of the same period except that they do not have front knobs. Each was fitted with a Chip-A-Way double cutter. They were made for Simmons by Ohio Tool Company.

The 1904 catalog states that Chip-A-Way planes have applewood blocks. However, it is very doubtful that the entire plane bodies were made of apple inasmuch as apple was always a premium wood. Other makers used apple in some cases for fancy planes such as panel plows but these planes were always quoted at a higher price than the standard beechwood varieties. Perhaps apple was used on these planes for the insert that is normally called a start or start pin.

Early Chip-A-Way logo

The catalogs are unclear as to the markings on this vintage of planes. The marking shown on the side of the plane in the illustrations is probably incorrect. Two examples have shown up with semi-circular saw-tooth logos as shown in the illustration; however, other types of marking may have also been used.

Although these planes are quite scarce, they are not in demand as name brand collectors items.

The following planes were offered during this period:

Smooth Plane.
8 1/4 inches long

Smooth Plane, handled.
10 1/2 inches long

Jack Plane.
16 inches long

Fore Plane.
22 inches long

Jointer Plane.
26, 28, 30 inches long

The same five types of bench planes as shown above, with a different Chip-A-Way logo, were offered from 1907 thru 1911. These planes were made of beechwood. The logo was incised on the double cutter as shown in the illustration and on the top surface of the plane body forward of the cutter. The letter designation does not appear on the hardware. Planes noted are 2 1/4 inches thick.

The following planes were offered during this time period:

Chip-A-Way cutter

CHS Smooth Plane, handled.
9 1/2 inches long

CS Smooth Plane.
8 inches long

CJ Jack Plane.
15 inches long

CF Fore Plane.
22 inches long

CP 26/28/30 Jointer Plane.
26,28,30 inches long

Although these planes are quite scarce, they are not in demand as name brand collectors items.

Chip-A-Way Metal and Wood Bottom Planes

A line of Chip-A-Way metal and wood bottom planes was listed in the 1911 Simmons price book under *New Goods* but was not mentioned in the 1912 general catalog. The price book illustrations are poor; however, the planes appear to be a second line similar to the first line Keen Kutter KK series.

The following planes were listed:

C/3 Smooth Plane
C/4 Smooth Plane
C/4C Smooth Plane
C/5 Jack Plane
C/5C Jack Plane
C/6 Fore Plane
C/6C Fore Plane
C/7 Jointer Plane
C/7C Jointer Plane
C/9 1/2 Block Plane
C/24 Smooth Plane, Wood Bottom
C/26 Jack Plane, Wood Bottom
C/27 Jack Plane, Wood Bottom
C/29 Fore Plane, Wood Bottom
C/35 Smooth Plane, Handled, Wood Bottom
C/101 Block Plane
C/102 Block Plane
C/103 Block Plane
C/110 Block Plane
C/120 Block Plane

Inasmuch as these planes were not included in later catalogs, it is considered doubtful if they exist. It is noted that Oak Leaf planes were offered as a second line starting in 1912.

Oak Leaf Planes

Oak Leaf logo used on Planes

A wide line of planes bearing the Oak Leaf logo was sold by Simmons Hardware Company. Oak Leaf was a registered trademark used on a large number of second quality tools including planes. The trademark was registered by Wm Enders Company and the words Wm Enders was often included as part of the logo. The logo is incised on the cutter of each plane.

Oak Leaf Wooden Planes $20 - $35 each

Wooden planes with the Oak Leaf logo were offered starting in 1912. These planes were made of beechwood and each was fitted with a double cutter. The logo was incised on the toe of each plane as well as on the cutter. The letter designation did not appear on the hardware.
The following planes were offered:

ES Smooth Plane.
Offered: 1912 thru 1929.
Length: 8 inches

EJ Jack Plane.
Offered: 1912 thru 1929.
Length: 15 inches 1912 - 1920, 16 inches 1921 and later

EHS Smooth Plane, handled.
Offered: 1912 thru 1914.
Length: 9 1/2 inches

EF Fore Plane.
Offered: 1912 thru 1929.
Length: 20 inches 1912 - 1920, 22 inches 1921 and later

EJP26/28/30 Jointer Plane.
Offered: 1912 thru 1923.
Length: 26, 28, 30 inches 1912 - 1916, 26 inches 1917 and later

Oak Leaf Metal and Wood Bottom Planes

Metal and wood bottom planes bearing the Oak Leaf logo were offered by Simmons starting in 1912. These were second quality planes similar to the Keen Kutter "K" series planes of the same period. All of the bench planes have double cutters and screw and lateral adjustment.

The metal bench planes have hardwood handles and knobs with cherry stain. The lever caps are polished. These planes have the numerical designation (i.e. No. 3) embossed on the casting.

The wood portions of the wood bottom planes are made of beechwood. The lever caps on these planes are japanned. The wood bottom planes noted have the plane number (i.e. No. 26) incised on the toe end.

The following planes were offered:

E2 Cabinet Scraper $15 - $25.
Offered: 1913 thru 1934.
Length: 12 1/2 inches. Handle: Beechwood

E3, E4, E4C Smooth Plane $25 - $45.
Offered: 1912 thru 1929

E5, E5C, E6, E6C Plane $25 - $40.
Offered: 1912 thru 1929.

E7, E7C Jointer Plane $35 - $60.
Offered: 1912 – 1920.

E9 1/2 Block Plane $25 - $40.
Offered: 1912 thru 1929

E24 Smooth Plane, Wood Bottom $25 - $40
Offered: 1912 thru 1929.

E26, E28 Plane, Wood Bottom $25 - $40.
Offered: 1912 thru 1929

E27, E29 Plane, Wood Botton $30 - $45.
Offered: 1912 thru 1920

E35 Smooth Plane, Handled, Wood Bottom $25 - $40.
Offered: 1912 thru 1929

E77 Cabinet Scraper $25 - $40.
Offered: 1912 thru 1934

E101 Block Plane $35 - $50.
Offered: 1912 thru 1929

E102 Block Plane $20 - $30.
Offered: 1912 thru 1929

E103 Block Plane $20 - $30.
Offered: 1912 thru 1929

E110 Block Plane $20 - $30.
Offered: 1912 thru 1929

E120 Block Plane $20 - $30. Offered:
1912 thru 1929

Cabinet Scraper $20 - $30.
Offered: 1917 thru 1934
Size: Offered in five sizes

Bay State Planes

Bay State Planes $15 to $25 each

Wooden planes having a Bay State label were offered by Simmons Hardware Company from 1917 thru 1920. They were made of beechwood. These were third quality planes prices below the Keen Kutter and the Oak Leaf brands. They replaced the low priced Ohio Tool Company brand offered under the Scioto trademark.

Smooth Plane.
Length: 8 inches.
Cutter: Single and double

Jack Plane.
Length: 16 inches.
Cutter: Single and double

Jointer Plane.
Length: 26 inches.
Cutter: Double

Nothing is known about these planes except the basic catalog data.

Bay State planes are scarce inasmuch as they were offered for such a short time. However, they are not widely known and therefore are not in demand as Simmons Hardware Company trademark collectibles.

Bailey's Blued Planes

A line of metal planes under the heading of *Bailey's Blued* were first listed in a late 1899 Simmons catalog. The name was claimed as a Simmons special brand. From the illustrations, it appears that these planes were identical to the Stanley line. The catalog states that they were copper plated and then blued to a beautiful finish. It is assumed that they were made for Simmons by Stanley Rule and Level Company.

A Bailey's Blued plane has never been identified.

The following planes were listed:

No. 03 Smooth 1899 thru 1903
No. 04 Smooth 1899 thru 1903
No. 05 Jack 1899 thru 1903
No. 06 Fore 1899 thru 1903
No. 07 Jointer 1899 thru 1903
No. 08 Jointer 1899 thru 1903
No. 018 Block, Knuckle Joint 1899 thru 1909
No. 019 Block, Knuckle Joint 1899 thru 1909

Spoke Shaves

Simmons Hardware Company offered four types of Keen Kutter spoke shaves starting in 1907. Four types of second quality shaves bearing the Oak Leaf mark were offered starting in 1913.

Keen Kutter "KK" Spoke Shaves

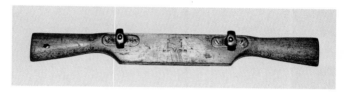

KK90 Spoke Shave, Wooden

KK90 Spoke Shave, Wooden $65 - $95
Offered: 1907 thru 1920
Length: 11 1/4 inches 1907 thru 1913, 10 1/2 inches 1914 and later. 11 inches observed
Width of Cutter: 2 7/8 inches 1907 thru 1916, 3 inches 1917 and later. 2 3/4 inches observed
Material: Beechwood
Faceplate: Steel 1907 thru 1912, Brass 1913 and later
Logo on the Wood: Wedge and Bar, St. Louis, U.S.A.
KK90 incised below the logo
Two brass thumbscrews provide for retention and adjustment of the cutter.
The 1914 and later catalogs show a hole in the left handle

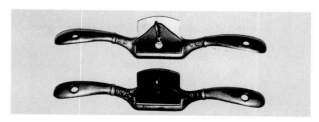

KK92 Spoke Shave, Straight

KK92 Spoke Shave, Straight $55 - $80
    Offered: 1907 thru 1913
    Length: 10 1/4 inches
    Width of Cutter: 2 1/8 inches
    Finish: Japanned frame with nickel plated handles 1907 thru 1909, nickel
        plated with frosted frame and polished handles 1910 and later
    Logo on the Cutter: Wedge and Bar, St. Louis, U.S.A.
    KK92 embossed on the top of the casting
    There are holes in both handles.
    There are two logos on the cutter in some cases

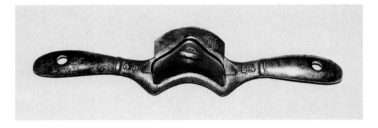

KK94 Spoke Shave, Concave

KK94 Spoke Shave, Concave $55 - $80
    Offered: 1907 thru 1913
    Length: 9 3/4 inches
    Width of Cutter: 2 1/4 inches
    Finish: Japanned frame with nickel plated handles 1907 thru 1909, nickel
        plated with frosted frame and polished handles 1910 and later
    Logo on the Cutter: Wedge and Bar, St. Louis, U.S.A.
    KK94 embossed on the top of the casting
    There are holes in both handles
    Those observed have only one logo on the cutter

KK96 Spoke Shave, Straight and Concave

KK96 Spoke Shave, Straight and Concave $65 - $95
    Offered: 1907 thru 1913
    Length: 12 1/4 inches

Width of Cutter: Straight 2 inches. Concave 2 1/8 inches, 2 1/4 inches
observed
Finish: Japanned frame with nickel plated handles 1907 thru 1909, nickel
plated with frosted frame and polished handles 1910 and later
Logo on the Cutter: Wedge and Bar, St. Louis, U.S.A.
KK96 embossed on the top of the casting
There are holes in both handles
There are two logos on each cutter in some cases

Keen Kutter "K" Spoke Shaves

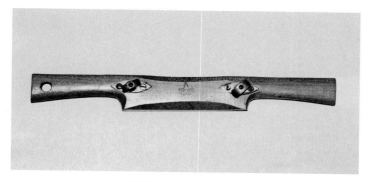

K90 Spoke Shave, wooden

K90 Spoke Shave, Wooden $70 - $100
Offered: 1921 thru 1923
Length: 10 1/2 inches. 11 1/4 inches observed
Width of Cutter: 3 inches
Material: Beechwood
Faceplate: Brass
Logo on the Wood: Wedge and Bar
Two brass thumbscrews provide for retention and adjustment of the cutter
There is a hole in the left handle

K91 Spoke Shave, straight

K91 Spoke Shave, Straight $50 - $75
    Offered: 1914 thru 1934
    Length: 10 1/4 inches
    Width of Cutter: 2 1/8 inches
    Finish: Japanned
    Logo on the Cutter: Wedge and Bar
    K91 embossed on the bottom of the casting and Keen Kutter embossed
    on the top
    There are holes in both handles
    The catalog illustrations are not correct

K95 Spoke Shave, concave

K95 Spoke Shave, Concave $50 - $75
    Offered: 1914 thru 1934
    Length: 9 3/4 inches
    Width of Cutter: 2 1/2 inches. 2 1/4 inches observed
    Finish: Japanned
    Logo on the Cutter: Wedge and Bar
    K95 embossed on the bottom of the casting and Keen Kutter embossed
    on the top
    There are holes in both handles
    The catalog illustrations are not correct

K97 Spoke Shave, straight and concave

K97 Spoke Shave, Straight and Concave $65 - $95
    Offered: 1914 thru 1929
    Length: 10 1/4 inches 1914 thru 1916, 9 7/8 inches 1917 and later
    Width of Cutters: 1 1/2 inches

Finish: Japanned
Logo on Each Cutter: Wedge and Bar
K97 embossed on the bottom of the casting and Keen Kutter embossed on the top
There are holes in both handles

Oak Leaf Spoke Shaves $40 - $65

Spoke Shave, straight.
Offered: 1913

Spoke Shave, straight.
Offered: 1914

Spoke Shave, straight.
Offered: 1915 thru 1929

Spoke Shave, concave.
Offered: 1913

Spoke Shave, adjustable throat.
Offered: 1913

Spoke Shave, straight and concave.
Offered: 1913 and 1914

Spoke Shave, straight and concave.
Offered: 1915 thru 1917

Spoke Shave, straight and concave.
Offered: 1918 thru 1929

Spoke shaves offered under the Oak Leaf brand have the logo on the cutters only. The base castings are not marked. There are holes in both handles. They have a japanned finish.

Plane Related Items

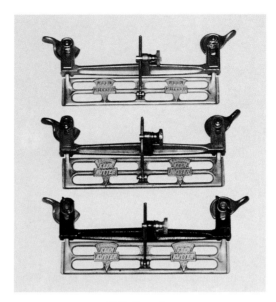

K55 Plane Gauge

K55 Plane Gauge, Keen Kutter $80 - $110
  Offered: 1912 thru 1929
  Length: 9 inches
  Finish: Nickel plated
  No 55 embossed on the casting

This device can be attached to any iron or wooden jack, fore, or jointer plane. It will guide the plane to cut a bevel at any angle or to square up the edge of a workpiece with maximum accuracy

Three varieties have been identified. The early variety has *Keen Kutter* only within the logo. See first illustration. Part of the latest variety is painted black

Rear handles for bench planes were offered by Simmons starting in 1910. These handles were intended for replacement purposes on Keen Kutter planes. They have the wedge and bar logo incised on the left side.

The following handles were listed: $25 - $35

KH3 Will fit planes KK3, KK3C, KK4, KK4C, KK10 1/2
  Offered: 1910 thru 1919
  Material: Rosewood

KH5 Will fit planes KK4 1/2 thru KK8C, and KK10
  Offered: 1910 thru 1919
  Material: Rosewood

Keen Kutter Plane Handle

KH26 Will fit all KK series wood bottom planes
    Offered: 1910 thru 1919
    Material: Beechwood

KH33 Will fit planes K3, K3C, K4, K4C, K10 1/2
    Offered: 1914 thru 1938
    Material: Rosewood

KH55 Will fit planes K4 1/2 thru K8C, and K10
    Offered: 1914 thru 1938
    Material: Rosewood

KWH26 Will fit K series wood bottom planes K26 thru K34
    Offered: 1914 thru 1938
    Material: Beechwood

Early catalogs state that the KH26 handle will fit all wood bottom planes. The catalogs failed to account for the shorter base of smooth planes KK35 and KK36

No. 40 Box Scraper, Keen Kutter

No. 40 Box Scraper, Keen Kutter $30 - $50
    Offered: 1895 thru 1920
    Length: 11 inches
    Width of Blade: 2 1/4 inches
    Logo on the Blade: Wedge and Bar 1907 and later
    The handle is made of hickory with a rosewood finish
    Listed as being suitable for use on butcher blocks

B1 Box Scraper, Bay State $20 - $35
    Offered: 1912 thru 1934   B1 Box Scraper, Bay State
    Length Overall: 7 inches
    Width of Blade: 5 1/4 inches
    The handle is made of hardwood with a plain finish

Prices

The plane prices shown are retail values of collectible tools. The top value is for a tool that is in essentially new condition without any rust or any evidence of use. The bottom value is for a tool that has been used but not abused or worn out. A tool at the bottom price should have more than half of the paint intact and very little, if any, pitting of the metal. A tool at the lower end can have minor problems with the wood such as nicks or a cracked handle but cannot have any chips or cracks in the metal parts. Repainting detracts from the value of a tool in almost every case.

Any tools with major parts missing, improper parts installed, badly pitted metal or cracks in the metal parts are not collectors items per se and should be priced below the minimum value shown. Such tools are often bought for parts with the intent of putting two or more poor items together to make one collectible tool.

A tool that is new in the original box will demand a premium price from most collectors. Such tools are quite scarce and difficult to appraise. However, twenty five percent above the upper value is the correct ballpark to be considered. This assumes, of coarse, that the box is also in nice condition. Torn, dirty or partial boxes have less value according to condition.

When either buying or selling, proper valuation of a tool is an important part of collecting. Condition, condition and condition are the three most important factors to consider after the tool has been identified.

The most common error in using any price guide is looking only at the top value in the price range. The top price should be used only for a tool in new or near new condition. Such a tool is always scarce.

Fakes and Phonies

Every Keen Kutter collector knows that there are many fakes, reproductions and other phony items being offered at flea markets, malls and auctions. *Let the Buyer Beware* is a good maxim for any collector.

Keen Kutter planes have not been reproduced in quantity at this point. Only two questionable planes have been identified. Scams involving planes have generally been limited to replacing or substituting parts on or from genuine Keen Kutter items. It takes a sharp eye and considerable knowledge of the subject to avoid buying a cobbled-up plane some part of which is marked with the Keen Kutter name or logo.

It is recommended that buyers keep the following thoughts in mind when buying a Keen Kutter plane:

- A Keen Kutter cutter in an unmarked plane of some other brand can sometimes fool even an advanced collector.
- A non-standard or unmarked cutter in a Keen Kutter plane is easy to detect but is often a simple attempt at fraud. Genuine Keen Kutter cutters are **always** marked.
- Lever caps are often replaced or interchanged. Such replacements can easily confuse most beginners.
- Planes having replaced or missing parts such as handles, knobs and screws are often seen. Any non-standard part will always reduce the value.
- When in doubt, review the descriptive material in this book.

Acknowledgements

The Author gratefully acknowledges assistance and/or information provided by:
Kelly Harms, Newton, Kansas
Jerry Heuring, Scott City, Missouri
Drake Shaw, Overland Park, Kansas
Woody Underwood, Mt. Hope, Kansas

Bibliography

Carroll, James A., *Fifty Stepping Stones in Hardware Business*, 1932
Carroll, James J., *He was the Greatest Sales Manager the Business World Ever Produced*, 1924
Dann, A. E., *History of the Simmons Hardware Company*, 1921
Edwards, Larry and Linda, *Shapleigh Hardware Diamond Edge, An Illustrated Value Guide*, Copyright 1992
The Great American Hardware Story, Hardware Age, Vol. 212, No. 7 July 4, 1975
The Gristmill, A publication of the Mid-West Tool Collectors Association. The several articles regarding Keen Kutter and Simmons Hardware Company.
Heuring, Jerry and Elaine, *Collector's Guide to Keen Kutter*. Copyright 2000
Missouri Historical Society Museum Library, St. Louis, Missouri
Norvell, Saunders, *Forty Years of Hardware*, Hardware Age, 1924
City Directories, St. Louis, Missouri
Testimonial Letters, Simmons Hardware Company, March 1905
Williamson, Harold F., *Winchester, The Gun that Won the West*, Combat Forces Press, Copyright 1952
General Catalogs, Simmons Hardware Company 1880, 1883, 1887, 1891, 1895, 1899, 1904, 1908, 1912, 1913, 1914, 1915, 1917, 1918, 1921/22, 1924, 1927, 1930, 1935, 1939, 1940
Specialty Catalogs, Simmons Hardware Company
      1882 Tools, Light Machinery and Supplies
      1887 Tools, Light Machinery and Supplies
      1906 Planes and Plane Irons
      1907 New York City
      1910 Manual Training Blue Book
      1911 G-4 Price Book
      1913 Planes and Plane Irons
Catalogs, Shapleigh Hardware Company
      1940 General, updated to 1941
      1942 General
      1951 Tool Catalog
      1958 Salesman's Catalog, updated
Simmons Hardware Company Want Books
Plus a host of other sources not documented

Appendix A

Items marked Keen Kutter

The following articles are known to have been marked with the Keen Kutter name or logo:

Advertising Items (Give-A-Ways)

Balloon
Calendar
Circular
Cuff Links*
Hand Fan
Hat
Key Chain
Kite
Lapel Pin*
Letter Opener*
Match Book*
Match Holder
Painters' Cap*
Paper Weight*
Pen, Ball Point
Pen, Fountain
Pencil, Bullet
Pencil, Carpenters'
Pencil, Grease
Pencil, Lead
Pencil, Mechanical
Pencil Clip*
Pinback Button
Pocket Notebook
Pocket Protector**
Pot Holder
Puzzle
Ruler
Screw Driver
Service Bulletin
Tie Tac *
Watch Fob*
Yard Stick*
Adze,
    House Carpenters'
    Railroad
    Ship Carpenters'
Airplane
Alarm Clock*
Anvil, Blacksmiths'
Anvil, Miniature*
Apple Parer
Apron, Carpenters'*
Auger, Nut
Automobile Casing (tire)
Automobile Inner Tube
Awl, Brad
Awl, Scratch
Awl and Tool Set
Axe,
    Boy Scout
    Boys'
    Broad*

    Campers'
    Coal Miners'
    Double Bit
    Firemen's or Fire Engine
    Freighters'
    House
    Hunters'
    Ice
    Scout
    Ship
    Single Bit
    Tommy
Axe Sheath
Bevel Protractor
Bicycle Tire
Bill Hook
Bit,
    Auger
    Car
    Countersink
    Electricians' or Bell Hangers'
    Expansive
    Gimlet
    Masonry **
    Reamer
    Screw Driver
    Screw Driver Set
    Ship Auger
    Ship Car
    Spade**
    Twist Drill or Bit Stock Drill
    Wood
Bit Brace,
    Corner
    Corner Ratchet
    Ratchet Drill
Bit Extension
Bit Set,
    Auger
    Twist Drill
    Wood
Boot Jack, Lobster *
Boring Machine
Bush or Brush Hook
Butt Gauge
Butter Spreader
Calipers, Inside
Calipers, Outside
Campers' Outfit
Can Opener
Cart, Yard
Carving Tool Set, Table
Carving Tool Set, Wood

Carving Tool, Wood
Cement Tool,
    Corner
    Edger
    Float
    Groover
    Indentation Roller
    Jointer
    Radius
Chain Drill Attachment
Chisel,
    Box
    Butt
    Cape
    Cold
    Corner
    Firmer
    Framing
    Mortising
    Putty
    Turning
    Wrecking
Chisel Roll
Chisel Set
Chopper, Butchers'
Cigarette Lighter*
Clamp, Hand Screw
Cleaver, Butchers'
Cleaver, Household
Clippers,
    Fetlock
    Hand Power
    Horse
    Nail
    Toilet
Cookbook
Cork Screw
Corn Mill
Corn Sheller
Corundum Wheel
Cotter Pin Lifter
Cotton or Box Hook
Crack Filler (for floors)
Cutlery Set,
    Childs'
    Kitchen
    Table
Crate Opener
Dental Snips
Desk Set (cutlery)
Display for a Float
Ditch Bank Blade
Dividers
Drain Cleaner
Drill,
    Breast
    Hand
    Hand, Automatic
    Post
    Star
Drill Point

Electric Tools**
    Bench Grinder
    Blender
    Circular Saw
    Drill
    Hair Cutting Set
    Jig Saw
    Hedge Trimmer
    Saber Saw
Emery Cloth
Emery Paper
Fence Sign
File,
    Band Saw
    Bastard
    Cabinet
    Cant Saw
    Cross Cut Saw
    Flat
    Gin Saw
    Half Round
    Hand, Second Cut
    Hand, Smooth
    Hook Tooth Saw
    Knife
    Mill
    Nail
    Pit Saw
    Round
    Saw
    Saw, Handled
    Square
    Warding
    Wood
Fishing Line
Flashlight
Flashlight Battery
Flint Paper
Food or Meat Chopper
Forge
Forge Blower
Fork,
    Alfalfa
    Baling Press
    Barley
    Barn
    Coal
    Coal Scoop
    Coke
    Cold Meat
    Cooks' or Pot
    Cottonseed
    Dessert
    Digging
    Garden
    Grain
    Hay
    Header
    Manure
    Meat
    Mill

Oyster
Salad
Spading
Stone
Sugar Beet Scoop
Table
Vegetable Scoop
Grain Cultivator
Garden Plow
Garden Tool Holder
Garden or Seaside Tool Set
Garden Weeder
Gasoline Can
Gimlet
Glass Cutter
Gloves, Cotton
Gouge, Socket Firmer
Gouge, Turning
Grass Catcher
Grass Cutter
Grass Hook
Grinder, Tool
Grinder, Tool, Pedal
Grinder, Tool and Sickle
Grinding Paste
Grindstone, Family
Grindstone, Pedal
Hamburger Turner or Cake Server
Hammer,
    Ball Pein
    Ball Pein, Automobile
    Bill Posters'
    Blacksmiths'
    Box
    Brad
    Brick
    Drill Sharpening
    Farriers'
    Hand Drilling
    Macadam Cracking
    Nail
    Nail, Fulcrum
    Ripping
    Riveting
    Rounding
    Saw Setting
    Shoe
    Stone
    Stone Masons'
    Striking
    Tack
    Tinners'
    Tinners' Paneing
    Upholsterers'
Handle,
    Axe
    Adze
    Chisel
    Crosscut Saw
    Drifting Pick
    File

Fork
Hammer
Hand Saw
Hatchet
Hoe
Mattock
Pick
Plane
Post Hole Digger
Scoop
Shovel
Sledge or Maul
Spade
Hatchet,
    Barreling
    Box
    Broad or Bench
    Car Builders'
    Claw
    Flooring
    Half
    Hunters'
    Lathing
    Produce
    Rig Builders' or Oil Derrick
    Shingling
    Tobacco
Hatchet Sheath
Hoe,
    Baby Warren
    Corn
    Cotton
    Cultivator
    Eye
    Garden
    Garden Mattock
    Grub or Sprouting
    Hazel
    Italian Grape
    Mattock
    Meadow
    Mortar
    Onion or Beet
    Palmetto
    Planters'
    Pusher or Stable
    Railroad Scuffle
    Sagebrush
    Scuffle or Sidewalk
    Strawberry
    Sugar Beet
    Tobacco
    Weeding
Hollow Auger
Holster, Pistol
Hose Washer
Ice Pick
Ice Shave
Ink Eraser or Office Knife
Jug, Whiskey*
Key, Door

Key, Padlock
Knife,
       Asparagus
       Beet Topping
       Boning
       Bread
       Broom Corn
       Budding
       Butcher
       Butchering Set
       Butter
       Cane
       Canning
       Carving
       Cheese
       Chicken or Turkey Sticking
       Chip Carving
       Citrus Fruit
       Clam
       Cooks'
       Corn
       Cotton Sampling
       Cuticle
       Desk
       Dessert
       Drawing
       Farriers'
       Fish
       French Cooks'
       Fruit
       Fruit Slicer
       Glaziers'
       Grape
       Grape Fruit
       Halibut
       Ham Slicer
       Harvester or Maize
       Hay
       Hedge
       Household
       Hunting
       Key Chain
       Linoleum or Oil Cloth
       Lunch Slicer
       Mincing
       Orange
       Oyster
       Paper Hangers'
       Paring (kitchen or potato)
       Putty
       Ribbing
       Scout Outfit
       Scraping
       Shoe
       Skinning
       Slicer
       Sloyd
       Sticking
       Steak
       Steak Set
       Table
       Tobacco
       Utility or Vegetable
Knife Pick
Knife Purse
Knife Steel
Kraut Cutter
Ladle,
       Cream,
       Gravy
       Oyster
       Soup
Lamp Trimmer
Lantern, Flash**
Lantern Slide
Lawn Mower
Lawn Mower Blade**
Lawn Mower, Pony
Lawn Mower Shafts
Lawn Spud
Lawn Tractor**
Lawn Trimmer
Level, Metal
Level, Torpedo
Level, Wooden
Level Glass
Lineman's Climbers
Lineman's Tool Kit
Lubricator (oil can)
Lubricating Oil
Magazine Ad
Mallet
Manicure Set
Manure Hook
Marking Gauge, Metal
Marking Gauge, Wood
Marble*
Marble Bag*
Match Holder*
Mattock
Maul, Ship
Maul, Wood Choppers'
Meat Cutter
Minnow Bucket
Mirror, Etched*
Mirror, Pocket*
Mitre Box
Nail Nipper (fingernail)
Nail Puller
Nail Set
Nippers, Cutting
Office Supplies,
       Bill Head (invoice)
       Check Blank
       Credit Memorandum
       Envelope
       Letter Head
       Mail Order Blank
       Note Head
       Postcard
       Receipt Blank
       Shipping Box*

Shipping Tag
Statement of Account
Oil Bottle*
Oiler
Padlock*
Paint
Paint Brush
Pick,
- Coal Miners'
- Drifting
- Mill
- Miners'
- Poll
- Prospecting
- Quarry
- Railroad

Pick Eye
Pick Mattock
Pie Server
Pincers,
- Carpenters'
- Farriers' Nail Cutting
- Hoof Paring
- Shoeing

Pinch or Wrecking Bar
Pipe Cutter
Pipe Dies
Pipe Stock
Plane,
- Block
- Block, Double Ender
- Block, Knuckle Joint
- Carriage Makers' Rabbet
- Circular
- Combination
- Fore, Iron
- Fore, Wood Bottom
- Fore, Wooden
- Jack, Iron
- Jack, Wood Bottom
- Jack, Wooden
- Jointer, Iron
- Jointer, Wood Bottom
- Jointer, Wooden
- Rabbet
- Rabbet, Bullnose
- Rabbet and Block
- Rabbet and Filletster
- Scraper
- Scrub
- Smooth, Iron
- Smooth, Wood Bottom
- Smooth, Wooden
- Tonguing and Grooving
- Veneer Scraper

Plane Iron
Plane Gauge
Plasterers' Hawk
Pliers,
- Chain Nose
- Channel Lock
- Combination
- Diagonal Cutting
- Flat Nose
- Gas Pipe
- Lineman's
- Long Nose
- Milliners'
- Needle Nose
- Round Nose
- Side Cutting
- Water Pump
- Wire Cutting

Plumb Bob
Pocket Knife
- Boy Scout
- Hand Hammered
- Kan and Karpenter
- Karpenter
- Kattle
- Office
- Our Own Keen Kutter
- Physicians'
- Pruner
- Sea Scout
- Spey
- Tickler
- Vaquero

Pocket Watch*
Post Hole Auger
Post Hole Digger
Potato Hook
Propane Torch**
Punch,
- Center
- Leather
- Leather, Revolving
- Leather, Spring
- Machine
- Pin
- Prick
- Ticket or Conductors'

Rake,
- Brume
- Coal or Road
- Dandelion
- Garden
- Park
- Tar or Asphalt

Rasp,
- Cabinet
- Horse
- Horse, Tanged
- Shoe
- Shoe, Flat
- Wood, Flat
- Wood, Half Round

Razor,
- Corn
- Safety
- Straight

Razor Blade, Safety

Razor Hone
Razor Set, Safety
Razor Set, Straight
Razor Strop
Reamer
Ring*
Rivet Set and Header
Router, Closed Throat
Router, Open Throat
Rubber Hose
Rule,
    Board
    Boxwood
    Folding (zig-zag type)
    Log
    Steel
Salesman's Case
Saw,
    Back
    Butcher
    Cabinet
    Compass
    Coping
    Crosscut
    Dehorning
    Flooring
    Hack
    Hand
    Ice
    Keyhole
    Kitchen
    Metal Cutting
    Mitre Box
    Panel
    Pruning
    Rip
    Stair Builders'
    Wood (buck)
Saw Blade,
    Butcher
    Circular**
    Coping
    Hack
    Wood (buck)
Saw Clamp
Saw Jointer and Gauge
Saw Set
Saw Tool Set
Saws, Nest of
Scales, Family*
Scissors,
    Button Hole
    Electricians'
    Embroidery or Lace
    Floral or Grape
    Folding
    Ladies or Regular
    Manicure
    Nail
    Pedicure
    Pocket

    Trimming
Scissors Set
Scissors and Shears Set
Scoop,
    Breakdown
    Coal Yard
    Gravel
    Grain
Scraper,
    Box
    Cabinet
    Three Cornered (bearing)
Screw Driver,
    Cabinet
    Offset
    Machinists'
    Ratchet Spiral
    Sewing Machine
    Standard
Screw Pitch Gauge
Screw Plate Set (tap and die set)
Scythe,
    Grain
    Grain or Lawn
    Grass
    Weed and Bush
Scythe Snath
Sewing Machine
Sewing Machine Needles
Shears,
    Bankers' or Paper
    Barbers'
    Game Carving
    Grass
    Hedge
    Horse or Mule
    Kitchen
    Mule
    Pruning
    Roaching
    Sheep
    Tailors'
    Trimmer, Bent
    Trimmer, Straight
Shellac
Shingle Gauge
Shoe Horn
Shotgun
Shovel
    Boys' or Campers'
    Campers' or Floral
    Concrete
    Dirt
    Ditching
    Garden
    Irrigating
    Miners'
    Moulders'
    Rice
    Sewer Diggers'
Sidewalk Cleaner

Skutch, Brick Layers'
Sledge,
    Blacksmiths'
    Coal Miners'
    Stone
Slick
Spade,
    Ditching
    Drain
    Tiling
Spark Plug
Spatula
Speed Indicator
Splicing Clamp
Spoke Pointer
Spoke Shave, Metal
Spoke Shave, Wood
Spoon,
    Berry
    Bouillon
    Coffee
    Dessert
    Orange
    Soup
    Table
    Tea
Sprayer, Garden**
Square,
    Combination
    Framing or Rafter
    Mitre
    Sliding T Bevel
    Take-Down
    Try
    Try and Mitre
Stain
Staple Puller
Stone, Axe
Stone or hone,
    Gouge Slip
    Oil
    Pocket Knife or Pen Knife
    Scythe
Stone Hook
Store Displays and Fixtures
    Animated Figures
    Axe Rack
    Clock*
    Counter Top Case*
    Crepe Paper Banner
    Display Box, Pocket Knife
    Display Stand
    Nail and Staple Box
    Neon Sign
    Picture
    Poster*
    Roll Paper Holder
    Showcase*
    Showcase Card
    Store Sign*
    Tool Rack

Twine Holder
Window Display
Window Valence
Store Supplies
    Booklet
    Cardboard Box
    Catalog*
    Circular
    Electrotype
    Nail Box
    Order Pad
    Pamphlet
    Paper Bag
    Parcel Post Tape Measure
    Price Calculator
    Price Sticker
    Price Tag
    Price Ticket
    Shipping Tag
    Store Coat
    Store Hat
    Want Book
    Wrapping Paper
    Wrapping Twine
Street Car Sign
Stropper, Safety Razor
Sugar Shell
Tack Claw
Tape Line, Cloth
Tape Line, Steel
Thermometer
Thermos Bottle**
Thermos Jug**
Thistle or Dock Cutter
Tiller, Engine Driven**
Tinners' Snips
Tobacco Cutter
Tool Bag
Tool Cabinet
Tool Cabinet and Work Bench
Tool Case
Tool Chest
Tool Kit, Automobile
Tool Set
Tool Set, Automobile
Tool Set, Gift
Trammel Points
Tree Pruner
Tree Sign
Trowel,
    Brick
    Corner
    Garden
    Plastering
    Pointing
Turf Edger
Turning Gouge and Chisel Combination
Tweezers
Varnish
Vise,
    Blacksmiths'

Hand
Machinists'
Pipe
Waffle Iron
Wagon, Boys'
Wagon Umbrella
Wedge,
    Axe
    Coal Miners'
    Hammer or Hatchet
    Stave Makers'
    Wood Choppers'
Weed Cutter
Weeder, Dandelion
Weeder, Garden
Wheel Barrow
Wire Brush

Wood Filler Paste
Wood Saw Frame
Work Bench
Wrecking Bar, Carpenters'
Wrench,
    Adjustable S
    Alligator
    Alligator, Adjustable
    Angle (Crescent pattern)
    Automobile
    Bicycle
    End (engineers)
    Nut
    Pipe
    Screw
    Tap
    Tappet
    Textile and Machine

* Beware of fake
** Shapleigh or Val-Test

Appendix B

Examples of Trademark Registration

RENEWED

RE-RENEWED

UNITED STATES PATENT OFFICE

SIMMONS HARDWARE COMPANY, OF ST. LOUIS, MISSOURI

TRADE-MARK FOR PLANES AND PLANE-IRONS.

No. 53,685. **Statement and Declaration.** **Registered June 12, 1906.**

Application filed November 23, 1905. Serial No. 14,939. Used ten years.

STATEMENT.

To all whom it may concern:

Be it known that the SIMMONS HARDWARE COMPANY, a corporation duly organized and existing under the laws of the State of Missouri, and located in the city of St. Louis, in said State, and doing business at Ninth and Spruce streets, in the said city of St. Louis, has adopted for its use a trade-mark, of which the following is a description.

The trade-mark consists of the words "KEEN KUTTER" and a figure of wedge shape having three-sided projections at its sides and on which said words appear.

The trade-mark has been continuously used in the business of said corporation since the year 1868.

The class of merchandise to which the trade-mark is appropriated is tools and cutting instruments, and the particular description of goods comprised in said class upon which said trade-mark is used is planes and plane-irons.

The trade-mark is usually displayed on the packages containing the goods by placing thereon a printed label on which the same is shown, or it may be imprinted directly upon the goods or upon the packages in which the goods are packed for sale.

[L. S.] SIMMONS HARDWARE COMPANY.
By A. W. DOUGLAS,
Vice-Prest.

DECLARATION.

State of Missouri, city of St. Louis, ss:

ARCHER W. DOUGLAS, being duly sworn, deposes and says that he is vice-president of the corporation, the applicant named in the foregoing statement; that he believes the foregoing statement is true; that he believes that said corporation is the owner of the trade-mark sought to be registered; that no other person, firm, corporation or association, to the best of his knowledge and belief, has the right to use said trade-mark, either in the identical form or in any such near resemblance thereto as might be calculated to deceive; that said trade-mark is used by said corporation in commerce among the several States of the United States, and particularly between Missouri and all of the States west of

the Mississippi River; and that the description, drawing and specimens presented truly represent the trade-mark sought to be registered; and that the trade-mark has been in actual use as a trade-mark of the applicant or its predecessor from whom it derived its for ten years next preceding the passage of the act of February 20, 1905, and that to the best of his knowledge and belief such use has been exclusive.

ARCHER W. DOUGLAS.

Subscribed and sworn to before me, a notary public, this 21st day of September, 190

[L. S.] L. D. WHITE,
Notary Public.

134

No. 53,685.

TRADE-MARK

REGISTERED JUNE 12, 1906.

SIMMONS HARDWARE COMPANY.
PLANES AND PLANE IRONS.
APPLICATION FILED NOV. 23, 1905.

Attest:

Wm N Scott

Blanche Hogan

Proprietor:

Simmons Hardware Company

By Dwight F Davis

Attys

RENEWED

UNITED STATES PATENT OFFICE.

SIMMONS HARDWARE CO., OF ST. LOUIS, MISSOURI.

TRADE-MARK FOR CERTAIN CUTTING AND EDGE TOOLS.

No. 60,570. **Statement and Declaration.** **Registered Feb. 12, 190?**

Application filed May 17, 1905. Serial No. 5,902.

STATEMENT.

To all whom it may concern:

Be it known that the SIMMONS HARDWARE Co., a corporation duly organized and existing under the laws of the State of Missouri, and located in the city of St. Louis, said State, and doing business at Ninth and Spruce streets, in the said city of St. Louis, has adopted for its use the trade-mark shown in the accompanying drawing.

The trade-mark has been continuously used in our business since the year 1868.

The class of merchandise to which the trade-mark is appropriated is Class 20, Cutlery not included in Class 61 and edge-tools, and the particular description of goods comprised in said class upon which said trade-mark is used is hair-clippers, table-knives, table-forks, carvers, razors scissors, shears, butcher-knives, broom-corn knives, sticking-knives, skinning-knives, farrier-knives, hunting-knives, pocket-knives, augers, auger-bits, gimlet-bits, countersink-bits, reamer-b gimlets, chisels, gouges, drawing-kniv bench-planes, plane-irons, files, rasps, c ting-pliers, cutting-pincers, cutting-punch cold-chisels, box-scrapers, mincing-kni knife-edge can-openers, glass-cutters, adz hatchets, axes, wood-saw blades, choppe cleavers, grass-hooks, bush-hooks, h knives, corn-knives, mattocks, crosscut-sa handsaws, compass-saws, scythes, she shears, and horse-shears.

The trade-mark is usually displayed on packages containing the goods by plac thereon a printed label on which the sam shown, or it may be imprinted directly up the goods or upon the packages in which goods are packed for sale.

[L. S.] SIMMONS HARDWARE CO,
By J. E. SMITH,
Vice-Pres.

DECLARATION

State of Missouri, city of St. Louis, ss:

J. E. SMITH, being duly sworn, deposes and says that he is vice-president of the corporation, the applicant named in the foregoing statement; that he believes the foregoing statement is true; that he believes that said corporation is the owner of the trade-mark sought to be registered; that no other person, firm, corporation or association, to the best of his knowledge and belief, has the right to use said trade-mark, either in the identical form or in any such near resemblance thereto as might be calculated to deceive; that said trade-mark is used by said corporation in commerce among the several States of the United States, and particularly between Mis- souri and all of the States west of the Mis sippi river; and that the description, draw and specimens presented truly represent trade-mark sought to be registered; and t the trade-mark has been in actual use a trade-mark of the applicant or its predeces from whom it derived title for ten years n preceding the passage of the act of Februa 20, 1905, and that to the best of his kno edge and belief said use has been exclusiv

J. E. SMITH

Subscribed and sworn to before me, a tary public, this 11th day of May, 1905.
[L. S.] JOHN F. MULDOON,
Notary Public, City of St. Louis, Mo

TRADE-MARK.

REGISTERED FEB. 12, 1907.

SIMMONS HARDWARE CO.
CERTAIN CUTTING AND EDGE TOOLS.
APPLICATION FILED MAY 17, 1906.

KEEN KUTTER

Attest:
W. H. Scott
Nellie E. Alexander

Proprietor:
Simmons Hardware Co.
By Knight Bros.
Attys.

70,064. REPRESENTATION OF HEAD OF CUTTING TOOL. Registered July 28, 1908. , Simmons Hardware Company, St. Louis, Mo. Re-renewed July 28, 1948, to Shapleigh Hardware Company, St. Louis, Mo., a corporation of Missouri. SCREW DRIVER BITS, BIT BRACES, ETC. Class 23.

70,064. CERTAIN TOOLS. Registered July 28, 1908. Simmons Hardware Company, St. Louis, Mo. Renewed July 28, 1928, to Simmons Hardware Company, New Haven, Conn., a Corporation of Missouri.

THIRD RENEWAL

VAL-TEST DISTRIBUTERS, INC
CHICAGO, ILL.

UNITED STATES PATENT OFFICE.

SIMMONS HARDWARE COMPANY, OF ST. LOUIS, MISSOURI.

TRADE-MARK FOR CERTAIN TOOLS.

No. 70,064. Statement and Declaration. Registered July 28, 1908.

Application filed June 10, 1907. Serial No. 28,015.

STATEMENT.

To all whom it may concern:

Be it known that the SIMMONS HARDWARE COMPANY, a corporation duly organized and existing under the laws of the State of Missouri, and having an office in the city of St. Louis, said State, and doing business at Ninth and Spruce streets, in the city of St. Louis, State of Missouri, has adopted for its use the trade-mark shown in the accompanying drawing.

The trade-mark has been continuously used by said corporation since November 11, 1905.

The class of merchandise to which the trade-mark is appropriated is Class 13, Hardware and plumbing and steam fitting supplies, and the particular description of goods comprised in said class upon which said trade-mark is used is screw driver bits, bit braces, brace jaws, carpenters' wrecking bars, screw drivers, putty knives, ice picks, post hole diggers, hammers, hoes, hay forks, header forks, manure forks, garden forks, potato hooks, manure hooks, metal handling ladles, picks, pick eyes, non-cutting carpenters' and blacksmiths' pincers, hand rakes, sledges, shovels, rivet sets, nail sets, saw sets, saw clamps, saw frames, implements for the laying and finishing of graniteoid, cement and mortar, garden trowels, awls, coal wedges, woodchoppers' wedges, nail pullers, non-cutting tools of awl and tool sets, and woodchoppers' mauls.

The trade-mark is used by printing it upon labels attached to the goods.

SIMMONS HARDWARE COMPANY.
By A. W. DOUGLAS,
Vice President.

DECLARATION.

State of Missouri: city of St. Louis: ss.:

ARCHER W. DOUGLAS, being duly sworn, deposes and says that he is vice president of the corporation, the SIMMONS HARDWARE COMPANY, having its office in the city of St. Louis, and State of Missouri, the applicant in the application for trade-mark registration filed June 10, 1907, Serial No. 28,015; that he believes the statement hereto attached is true; that he believes said corporation is the owner of the trade-mark sought to be registered; that no other person, firm, corporation or association, to the best of his knowledge and belief, has the right to use said trade-mark, either in the identical form or in any such near resemblance thereto as might be calculated to deceive; that said trade-mark is used by said corporation in commerce among the several States of the United States; that the drawing presented truly represents the trade-mark sought to be registered; and that the specimens show the trade-mark as actually used upon the goods.

ARCHER W. DOUGLAS.

Subscribed and sworn to before me, a notary public, this 14th day of April 1908.

[L. S.] WALTER J. G. NEUN,
Notary Public.

138

No. 70,084.

REGISTERED JULY 28, 1908.

SIMMONS HARDWARE COMPANY.
CERTAIN TOOLS.
APPLICATION FILED JUNE 10, 1907.

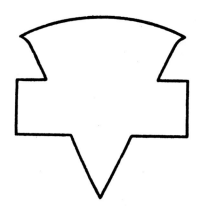

Attest:

Wm. H. Scott

Lily Rust

Proprietor:

Simmons Hardware Company,

By

R. Knight Atty.

Three examples of Keen Kutter trademark application and registration are shown. The first one registers the use of the Keen Kutter logo for use on planes and plane irons only. The second one applies the name Keen Kutter without the logo shape and the third example registers the logo shape without the words Keen Kutter.

Appendix C

Examples of Keen Kutter Marks

Pocket Knife 1880

Butcher Knife 1883

Sheep Shears 1883

Auger Bit Box 1887

Saw 1883

Trowel 1887

Hand Fan 1904

Black Jack Maul 1907

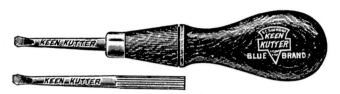

Blue Brand Brad Awl 1907

Expert Trowel 1907

Special Bit Box 1907

Sure Grip Wrench 1910

Paint 1930

Wrapping Paper 1930

Automobile Tires 1935

Appendix D

Special Brands

The following special brand names were used by Simmons Hardware Company:

ACCOMAC - Fishing leader
ACME - Bird cage assortment
AETNA - Numerous items
AFRICAN STEEL CANE - Fishing rod
AGRICULTURAL - Leather belting
AIRTITE - Bicycle tire, refrigerator (icebox)
A. LATHAM'S KANSAS - Hand saw
ALL-RIGHT - Lamp assortment
AMERICAN - Sporting goods
AMERICAN ACADEMIC - Football, basketball
AMERICAN AMATEUR - Baseball, football
AMERICAN ASSOCIATION - Baseball
AMERICAN BAT COMPANY - Baseball bat
AMERICAN COLLEGIATE - Football, basketball
AMERICAN EXPRESS - Boys' wagon
AMERICAN FLYER - Baseball
AMERICAN HIGH SCHOOL - Football
AMERICAN INTERCOLLEGIATE - Football
AMERICAN INVINCIBLE - Fishing line
AMERICAN LEADER - Baseball bat
AMERICAN LEAGUE - Baseball, baseball bat
AMERICAN LINE COMPANY - Fishing line
AMERICAN MITTEN COMPANY - Catchers' mitt
AMERICAN OFFICIAL - Sporting goods
AMERICAN OFFICIAL ACADEMIC - Football
AMERICAN OFFICIAL ASSOCIATION - Football
AMERICAN OFFICIAL CANADIAN - Football
AMERICAN OFFICIAL COLLEGIATE - Football
AMERICAN OFFICIAL GAELIC - Football
AMERICAN OFFICIAL INTERCOLLEGIATE - Football
AMERICAN PRACTICE - Basketball, football
AMERICAN SCHOLASTIC - Football
AMERICAN SPECIAL - Sporting goods
ANTI-FRICTION - Axle grease
ANTLERS - Fishing float, fish hook
ARANSAS PASS - Fish hook
ARISTOCRAT - Fishing line
ARIZONA SPECIAL - Cartridge belt
ARKANSAS - Froe, hoe, wedge
ARKANSAS RATTLER - Razor
ASH - Baseball bat
ATLANTIC - Fishing line
AUNT NANCY - Coffee mill, sad iron
AXTELL - Horse rasp
BABY HAMMERLESS - Revolver
BADGER - Fishing line
BAILEY'S BLUED - Plane
BAKE FAST - Kitchen range, camp stove
BALL BALANCED - Baseball bat
BALTIC - Packing, rubber belting, hose
BANNER - Numerous items
BANNER MILLS - Fishing equipment
BARBERS' PET - Razor, razor strop
BASS - Brush, baseball bat
BASTILE - Padlock

BAY STATE - Numerous items
BEAUTY - Kitchen range
BEFORE THE WAR QUALITY - Razor strop
BELFAST - Fishing line
BERKSHIRE - Fishing line
BERLIN BLUE - Churn, enameled ware
BEST - Hame strings
BEST OF ALL - Razor
BIG BOY - Horse collar
BIRD - Bicycle
BISCAYNE BAY - Fishing line, fishing reel
BISHOP also L. BISHOP'S - Grass shears, axe
BISON - Rubber belting
BLACK BEAUTY - Padlock, paint brush

BLACK CHIEF - Stove polish, shoe polish, brush
BLACK DIAMOND - Coffee mill
BLACK HAWK - Paint brush

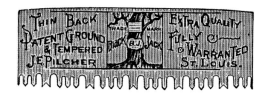

BLACK JACK - Tools
BLACK SNAKE - Crosscut saw
BLUE - Tape line, stovepipe, pencil
BLUE BEAM - Scales
BLUE BIRD - Washboard, bicycle
BLUE BLAST - Stove pipe, elbow
BLUE BRAND also B-B - Tools

BLUE GRASS - Grass shears
BLUE JAY - Oiler
BLUE OAK - Axe handle
BONANZA - Razor
BOSS - Jack screw, boys' wagon, knife
BOYS' AMATEUR - Baseball
BOYS' FAVORITE - Saw
BRADSHAW - Cutlery
BRIGHTEST & BEST also B & B - Stove
BRILLIANT - Shovel
BRITE-LITE - Gas mantle
BROOKLINE - Fishing line
BROWN'S - Shovel, needles
BUCK - Washboard
BUCKEYE - Corn knife, coffee mill
BUCKTHORN - Saw blade

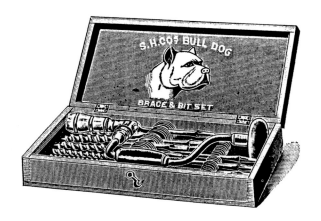

BULL-DOG - Tool set, padlock
BULLS EYE - Padlock
BULLY BOY - Baseball
BUTTER CUP - Brush
CALIFORNIA - Shovel
CALUMET CASTING - Fishing reel
CANNON BREECH - Gun
CAN'T B BEAT - Hand saw
CARNATION PATTERN - Tableware
CARPENTERS' SPECIAL - File
CARRARA - Paint
CARR'S - Shovel
CASTALIA - Fishing line, fishing reel
CASTALIA CASTING - Fishing line, fishing reel
CASTLEN - Shovel, spade
CATARACT - Rubber hose
CENTURY - Wringer, boxing gloves
CHALLENGE - Shovel
CHAMPION - Axe handle, lawn tennis ball
CHAMPIONSHIP - Lawn tennis racket
CHEYENNE - Buggy whip
CHIEF - Horse collar
CHIP-A-WAY - Tools, cutlery

CLASSIC - Kitchen range
CLAYBANK - Scoop, road scraper, shovel
CLEAN GLOSS - Furniture polish
CLEAR HIDE - Leather belting
CLIMAX - Stove polish, croquet set
CLIPPER - Numerous items
COATES - Fetlock clipper
COCOA HANDLE - Pocket knife
COLONIAL - Lamp assortment
COLORADO - Axe handle, shovel
COLUMBIA - Numerous items
COMET - Dry battery, baseball
COMFORT - Wringer
COMMON SENSE - Horse collar
COMPETITION - Cotton twine
COMPETITIVE - Buggy wood
CONQUEROR - Saw
COONEY CASTING - Fishing line
COONEY SPECIAL - Fishing line
CORNELL FIRE ARMS COMPANY - Shotgun
COWBOY - Coffee mill, rope
CQR - Padlock
CRACKER JACK - Baseball, horse collar
CREPELINE - Toilet paper
CRESCENT - Shovel
CRESUS - Horse clipper
CROCODILE - Brush
CROSSTIE SPECIAL - Adze
CROWN - Numerous items
CROWN BRAND - Cartridge belt, scabbard, holster
CRYSTAL ZINC - Washboard
CUCUMBER - Wooden pump
CUMBERLAND - Axe, tool handle
CUMBERLAND 49ER - Pick handle
CUT-I-CURE-U - Buck saw
CUTLASS - Scythe stone
DAISY - Lamp burner
DAMASCUS - Razor
DANDY - Horse collar, lamp assortment
DAZZLER - Washboard, pencil
DEAD SHOT - Mouse trap, rat trap, gun

DEER FOOT - Paint, liquid polish
DEFIANCE - Numerous items
DELIGHT - Wringer
DELFT - Enameled ware
DELMAR - Numerous items
DELMONICO - Enameled ware
DEPENDABLE - Bicycle tire
DE SOTO - Padlock, tin plate
DEXTER - Bicycle tire, horseshoe nails, seine
DIAMOND - Baseball
DISCOVERY - Lamp assortment
DIXIE - Padlock, seine
DOE RUN - Shovel
DOLLAR DEAD - Baseball
DOLPHIN - Rubber hose
DOMESTIC - Lamp assortment
DOUBLE BOTTOM - Coal hod, road scraper
DOUBLE HANDLE - Stove shovel
DOUBLE PROTECTOR - Washboard
DRAKE - Brush
DRIVE WELL - Numerous items
DROP EASY - Corn planter
DUBLIN BASS - Fishing equipment
DUCHESS - Paint brush

DUCK BILL - Alligator wrench
DUKE - Paint brush
DUNWELL - Kitchen range
DUPLEX - Fishing line
DUPLEX BASS - Fishing reel
EAGLE - Wringer
EASY SHAVER - Razor
E. C. SIMMONS - Numerous items
E. C. SIMMONS CELEBRATED - Automatic screw driver
ECLIPSE - Numerous items
ECLIPSE BEAUTY - Gun
ECLIPSE COMET - Gun
ECLIPSE DANDY - Gun
ECLIPSE GIANT - Gun
ECLIPSE HAMMOCK COMPANY - Hammock
ECLIPSE HERCULES - Gun
ECLIPSE LEADER - Gun
ECLIPSE VICTOR - Gun
ECLIPSE WONDER - Gun
ECONOMY - Numerous items
EDDIE COLLINS - Baseball bat
E. F. - Cotton hose
ELECTRA - Gun
ELECTRIC - Washboard, paint brush
ELK - Padlock
EMBOSSED - Lamp assortment

EMPEROR - Paint brush, washboard
EMPRESS - Paint brush, washboard
ENDERS' also Wm. Enders' - Numerous items
ENDERS' DOLLAR - Safety razor
ENDERS' SPECIAL SERVICE - Shotgun
ESSEX - Wrench, wringer
EUREKA - Lawn rake, well bucket, bird cage
EURITH PATTERN - Tableware
EVERLASTING - Hames
EXCELSIOR - Razor
EXPERT - Sporting goods, saw, trowel
EXTRA GRADE - Pencil, thermometer, tape
EXTRA QUALITY - Tools
FALSTAFF - Playing cards
FAMOUS - Rubber hose, baseball
FARMER BOY - Numerous items
FARMERS' - Rivet set, tool handle
FAST MAIL - Saw, coal scoop, rubber hose
FAULTLESS - Shovel, wringer, gasoline can
FAVORITE - Saw rod, sewing machine oil
FELT-LESS JUNIOR - Sweat pad
FIDELITY - Cotton hose, lamp assortment
FINCH'S also H. M. FINCH'S - Tools
FIRESIDE - Lamp assortment
FLAXOID - Fishing line
FLORIDA - Fishing line
FONTENAC - Fishing line
FOREHAND ARMS COMPANY - Gun
FOREIGN - Whitewash brush
FORREST - Golf club
FORTUNE - Lamp assortment
FREIGHTERS' - Jack screw
FRINGE - Lamp assortment
GALVO - Stove pipe, elbow
GANDER - Brush
GARDEN STATE - Spade
GARNET - Padlock
GEM - Bait casting outfit
GENUINE RUSSIAN - Razor strop
GIANT - Grind stone, saw rod, stove
GIBSON - Turkey call
GLADSTONE - Dog collar
GLENDALE - Toilet paper, lawn tennis racket
GLENWOOD - Lawn tennis racket
GLENWOOD CLUB - Lawn tennis ball
GLENWOOD SPECIAL - Lawn tennis racket
GLOBE - Shears
GOLD - Bird cage
GOLD BAND - Lamp assortment
GOLD DUST - Axe
GOOD LUCK - Lamp assortment
GOOD SERVICE - Kitchen range
GRANDMA'S - Lamp assortment
GRAYLING - Fishing leader
GRAY ROCK - Enameled ware
GREENFIELD - Coffee mill
GREENHEART - Golf club
GRIP TITE - Bicycle tire
GULF TARPON - Fishing equipment
GUNNISON - Fishing leader
GUNOLINE - Gun grease

HAMLET - Playing cards
HAND HAMMERED - Pocket knife
HANDY - Husking glove, nippers, tool kit
HANDY COMBINATION - Washboard
HANS WAGNER - Baseball bat
HAPPY MEDIUM - Bucksaw
HARDWARE MAN'S - Pencil
HARRY DAVIS - Baseball bat
HARTFORD FIRE ARMS COMPANY - Shotgun
HAWKEYE - Corn knife
HELPING HAND - Sewing machine
HERCULES - Wheel barrow
HERO - Cotton twine
HEXAGON - Pencil
HIAWATHA - Fishing line
HI FLY - Baseball
HIGHEST QUALITY ENGLISH - Trout fly
HIGH GRADE - Seine, fish hook
HIGH TONE - Cow bell
HODB - Axe handle
HOLD ALL - Fishing leader
HOLD FAST - Step ladder, snap
HOLLAND SCENE - Lamp assortment
HOME RUN - Baseball, baseball bat
HOOSIER - Axe
HORNET - Cutlery, gas mantle
HORSE SENSE - Horse collar
HORSE SHOE BRAND - Paint
HOUSEHOLD - Lamp assortment
HOWARD also E.W. HOWARD - Tools, cutlery
HRDB - Axe handle
ICEBERG - Water cooler
IDEAL - Tool set
ILLINOIS - Hedge knife, hoe, spade
IMPERIAL - Sporting goods, buggy wood
INDEPENDENCE - Shovel
INGLESYDE - Toilet paper, lawn tennis items
INTERCHANGEABLE MARVEL - Gun
INVINCIBLE QUAD - Fishing reel
IRIS - Hair clipper
IRON DUKE - Hammer, wringer
JET BLACK - Axe
J. I. C - Horse shoe nails
J. I. C. RACER - Horse shoe nails
JUNIOR KOASTER - Boys' wagon
JUNIOR PROFESSIONAL - Baseball
JUPITER - Roofing plate, fishing reel
KAN AND KARPENTERS' KNIFE - Pocket knife
KANT LEAK - Gasoline can, oil can
KANT SKID - Bicycle tire
KAR KING - Rubber hose
KARPENTER KNIFE - Pocket knife
KARPET KING - Carpet sweeper, hammer
KATCH ALL - Fishing bait
KATTLE KNIFE - Pocket knife
KEEN KASTER - Fishing reel
KEEN KLIPPER - Lawn mower, oil, oiler, catcher
KEEN KOOKER - Kitchen range
KEEN KUTTER - Numerous items
KEEN KUTTER BALL BEARING - Pliers
KEEN KUTTER JUNIOR - Safety razor, razor hone

KEEN KUTTER KARVER - Knife
KEEN KUTTER KOMBINATION - Razor hone
KEEN KUTTER PRUNER - Pocket knife
KEEN KUTTER SCOUT - Pocket knife
KEEN TONE - Radio
KEEP KOOL - Babbitt metal, soldering copper
KEOGH'S - Sheep marking oil
KETCH - Padlock
KETCH-ALL - Fishing equipment
KETCH-EM - Fish bait
KEYSTONE - Farm and garden tools
KEYSTONE METAL - Table cutlery
KEYSTONE RED RIVER - Hoe
KILMARNOCK - Golf club varnish
KING also KING, JR. - Football
KING BEE - Numerous items
KING-KOASTER - Boys' wagon, sled
KING KORN - Padlock
KING OF THE DIAMOND - Baseball bat
KING OF THE FIELD - Baseball bat
KINGSWAY - Tires, tubes
KIN-KINNICK - Fishing leader
K K KORD - Automobile tire, automobile tube
K-K - Numerous items
K. K. - Sporting goods
K.K. PIGEON GUN - Gun
K.K. SPECIAL - Sporting goods
KLAY KING - Farm tools
KLEAN KILLER - Gun
KLEAN KWICK - Metal polish
KLEAR KRYSTAL - Lamp chimney
KLICKER - Numerous items
KLINCHER - Numerous items
KLIPPER - Lamp burner
KLIPPER KLUB - Ice skates
KLOVER KATCHER - Grass catcher
KNICKERBOCKER - Lawn tennis racket
KNOXALL - Numerous items
KOAL KING - Coal hod
KOASTER - Boys' wagon
KOBE - Fishing line
KOFFEE KRUSHER - Grinding mill
KON-KAVE - Drawing knife
KOONEY KASTING - Fishing line, fishing reel
KOO-CHOOK - Packing, rubber belting and hose
KOOL KING - Ice box
KORKER - Lamp assortment
KORN KING - Broom corn knife
KORN KNIFE - Pocket knife
KORN KRUSHER - Grinding mill
KORN RAZOR - Razor
KREOLE - Axe handle, brush, cane knife
KRUGER - Paint brush
KRYSTAL BLUED STEEL - Gun
LACLEDE - Numerous items
LACLEDE SPECIAL - Axe handle, wringer, gas mantle
LA NIXTAMALERA - Corn mill
LARCHMONT - Lawn tennis racket
LATHAM'S - Punch, shoe knife
LEADER - Numerous items
LEAGUE - Baseball, baseball bat

LIBERTY - Lantern, fount, burner, lamp
LIGHTNIN - Storage battery
LIGNITE - Stove
LILIPUTIAN - Washboard, razor
LILY WHITE WASHITA - Oil stone
LINEOID - Fishing line
LITTLE CLOUD - Buggy whip
LITTLE DIMPLE - Washboard
LITTLE DOT - Toy wringer
LITTLE GEM - Washboard
LITTLE GIANT - Numerous items
LITTLE PET - Gun
LITTLE PRINCE - Fishing line
LONE STAR - Axe handle, hoe, prod stick
LONG WEAR - Horse collar
LOTUS - Washboard
LOUISIANA - Cane knife
LOUISVILLE CASTING - Fishing reel
LOUISVILLE SLUGGER JR. - Baseball bat
LOUISVILLE YOUTHS' SLUGGER - Baseball bat
LUCERN - Scythe
MAGNOLIA - Babbitt metal
MAIL ORDER - Pencil
MAPLE - Baseball bat
MARINE - Rope
MARQUETTE - Toilet paper
MARVEL - Rifle, sewing machine
MASCOT - Fishing line, fishing reel
MASCOT CASTING - Fishing reel
MAYWELL - Horse collar
MAYNARD - Shovel, spade
MEIER'S - Tools
MENTOR - Padlock
MERAMEC - Roofing plate, rubber hose
MESQUITE - Axe
METEOR - Numerous items
MIDGET - Toy wringer
MILKMAN - Hand bell
MINNESOTA CHIEF - Axe handle, saw blade
MISSOURI - Padlock
MISSOURI EXTRA - Axe handle
MISSOURI MULE - Mule shears
MODEL - Lamp assortment
MOGUL - Scoop
MOHAWK - Lamp assortment
MONARCH - Numerous items
MONDAY - Wringer
MONITOR - Minnow bucket
MONTANA - Hay fork, saw blade, shovel
MOON STONE - Enameled ware, churn
MORTON'S - Spade
MOUND CITY STAR - Leather belting
MULE SENSE - Mule collar
MURDOCK - Rifle
MUSKEGON - Fishing leader
MUSTACHE - Fishing line
NAPOLEON - Paint brush
NAPOLEON LAJOIE - Baseball bat
NATIONAL - Numerous items
NEPIGON - Fishing leader
NEVER SLIP - Wrench

NEW DIXIE - Minnow seine
NEW DRIVEWELL - Horseshoe nails
NEW ERA - Gun
NEW HAVEN FIRE ARMS COMPANY - Shotgun
NEW IDEA - Striking bag platform
NEW NITRO - Gun
NEW ROYAL - Canvas goods
NIMBLE NICKEL - Carpet tacks
NITRO MARVEL - Gun
NO. 8 SPECIAL - Razor
NO. F - Cotton hose
NONPAREIL - Tool handle
NORMA PATTERN - Plated ware
NORTHAMPTON - Shovel
NORTHERN - Fishing equipment
NORTHERN QUEEN - Washboard
NORTH STAR - Axe stone, ice saw, grain scoop
NORVELL'S - Tools
NOXALL - Padlock
NUART - Fishing line
NUBIAN - Padlock
NUTWOOD - Horse cart
OAK LEAF - Numerous items
OAK LEAF RED RIVER - Hoe
OFFICE STANDARD - Pencil
OFFICIAL COLLEGE LEAGUE - Baseball
OHIO BOY - Corn knife, lawn rake
OHIO FALLS - Boys' axe, hatchet
OIL TEMPERED - Baseball bat
O. K. - Stove shovel
OLD DIXIE - Mattock
OLD ORIGINAL - Hog ringer
OLD SOL - Lamp burner
OLYMPIAN - Fishing line
OREGON - Sewing machine, lamp assortment
OREGON MIST - Fishing line
ORDO - Stove pipe
ORIENT - Lamp assortment
ORIENTAL - Toilet paper, lawn tennis racket
ORIENTAL EXPERT - Lawn tennis racket
ORIENTAL SPECIAL - Lawn tennis racket
OROIDE - Carpet tacks
OSWEGO CASTING - Fishing reel
OTHELLO - Playing cards
OUANANICHE - Fishing leader
OUR BEAUTY - Razor
OUR BOY - Pocket knife
OUR CLIPPER - Scythe, grain cradle
OUR FAVORITE - Hand saw
OUR LEADER - Scissors, shears
OUR OWN KEEN KUTTER - Pocket knife
OVERLAND - Scoop, chain
OVERLAND LOCOMOTIVE - Scoop
OZARK - Numerous items
PASTIME - Wringer
PEACH - Lamp assortment
PEERLESS - Gun cleaner, lamp, gas stove
PEGAMOID - Paint, leather dressing
PENNANT - Numerous items
PENNANT WINNER - Baseball
PEORIA OAK - Stove

PERFECT - Paint brush
PERFECTION - Numerous items
PICKANINNY - Baseball
PILCHER'S - Tools
PINCH HITTER - Baseball bat
POCOMOKE - Fishing leader
POLAR - Ice saw, water cooler
POLLY PRIM - Numerous items
POLYGRADE - Pencil
PON-HONOR - Numerous items
PONTIAC - Buggy whip
PONY BARLOW - Pocket knife
POPULAR - Carpet sweeper, cobblers' outfit
PORTER HOUSE - Butcher saw, saw blade
POTOMAC - Fishing leader
POWERS - Gun cleaning rod
PREMIER - Canvas goods, fishing equipment
PREPAREDNESS - Padlock
PRESIDENT - Razor
PRINCE - Paint brush
PROFESSIONAL - Baseball bat, lawn tennis racket
PROTECTOR - Washboard
PYRAMID - Padlock
QUAKER CITY - Hammock
QUALITY - Padlock
QUEEN - Wrench, wringer
QUEEN ANNE - Kitchen range
RADIUM - Wood heater
RAINBOW - Fishing leader, baseball
RANCHERO - Pocket knife
RANCHMEN'S - Horse shoes
RANGER - Baggage, horse equipment
RAPID - Razor strop
RATTLER - Razor, razor strop
RED BEAUTY - Lamp assortment
RED BIRD - Bicycle
RED COAT - Axe, hatchet
RED DEVIL - Baseball
RED DRAGON - Fishing line
RED JACKET - Hatchet
RED LINE - Folding rule, pencil
RED TOP - Scythe, grain cradle
RED W BRAND - Paint
RED WEST - Lariat rope
REDWOOD - Pencil
REFLECTION - Stove polish
REGAL - Wrapping paper, wringer
RELIABLE - Lamp assortment
RELIANCE - Rubber hose
ROBIN'S EGG - Kitchenware
ROCHESTER - Lamp
ROCKET - Baseball, toy wagon
ROLO - Numerous items
ROMEO - Playing cards
ROUGH AND READY - Scythe
ROUGH RIDER - Rifle
ROVER - Boys' wagon
ROYAL - Numerous items
ROYAL AMERICAN - Gun
ROYAL CELEBRATED - Razor
ROYAL DUKE - Gun

ROYAL FIELD - Gun
ROYAL JUNIOR - Gun
ROYAL MONARCH - Gun
ROYAL NONPAREIL - Hunting coat
ROYAL RANGE - Tent
ROYAL SERVICE - Gun
ROYAL WESTERN - Horse collar
ROYAL WINNER - Gun
ROYALTON - Table cutlery
RUBBER - Belting
RUB WELL - Washboard
RUN EASY - Numerous items

SAFETY FIRST - Padlock
SALAMANDER - Wood heater
SALMON - Fishing leader, brush
SALVABLE - Fetlock clipper
SAMSON - Numerous items
SANITAS - Refrigerator (ice box)
SARATOGA - Fishing line
SCOTCH SPECIAL - Fishing line
SCRATCH BOOK - Pencil
SELF-BALANCING - Cream separator
SEMPER IDEM - Shears
SENATOR - Razor, razor strop
SHAKESPEARE - Fishing Reel
SHAKESPEARIAN CARD COMPANY - Playing cards
SHAMROCK - Fishing line
S. H. COMPANY - Numerous items
SHENANDOAH PATTERN - Plated ware
SHORTHAND - Pencil
SIBERIA - Refrigerator (icebox)
SIMCO - Copying pencil
SIMMONS - Numerous items
SIMMONS AMATEUR LEAGUE - Baseball bat
SIMMONS AUTOCYCLE - Bicycle
SIMMONS BEST - Hame straps

SIMMONS BOY SCOUT - Bicycle
SIMMONS HARDWARE CO. - Numerous items
SIMMONS JUNIOR LEAGUE - Baseball, baseball bat
SIMMONS KRAFT - Wrapping paper
SIMMONS MAJOR LEAGUE - Baseball bat
SIMMONS OFFICIAL LEAGUE - Baseball
SINGLE BOTTOM - Coal hod
SMILEY'S - Numerous items
SMILEY'S DELIGHT - Hand saw
SNAP - Lamp assortment
SOLID GRIP - Husking glove
SOLID STEEL - Skillet, kettle
SOLID ZINC - Washboard
SONGSTER - Bird cage assortment
SONNY - Pocket knife
SOUTHERNER - Horse collar
SOUTHLAND - Horse collar
SPEAKER SPECIAL - Scoop
SPECIAL - Numerous items
SPIDER - Hair clipper
SPOKE - Brush
STANDARD - Thermometer, razor strop
STAR - Barrel churn, twine
STEADFAST - Step ladder
STEAM WASHER - Washing machine
STEDY-LITE - Flashlight, battery
STERLING - Numerous items
STEVENS' - Spade
ST. LOUIS - Numerous items
ST. LOUIS 1904 - Saw
STOCKTON'S - Tools
STRONGHOLD - Padlock, step ladder
STRONG'S - Shovel, spade
SUBLETT'S - Hoe, fork, bush hook
SUCTION GRIP - Bicycle tire
SUNSET - Horse shoes
SUPERB - Lamp assortment
SUPERIOR - Canvas goods, razor, tire tape
SURE GRIP also S. G. - Numerous items
SURE LOCK - Stove pipe
SURPRISE - Minnow trap
SUWANNEE - Mattock, shovel
SWAN - Minnow bucket
SWATTER - Baseball bat
SWEDISH - Razor
SWEEPSTAKES - Handsaw
SWIFT - Hand saw, hair clippers, saw set
TAAK-ME - Fishing line
TALLY-HO - Hoe
TARPON - Wire brush
TEXAS - Wedge
THIN BACK - Crosscut saw
THISTLE PATTERN - Table ware
THOMLINSON - Gun cleaner
TOGO - Padlock
TOKIO - Fishing line
TORNADO - Rubber belting
TOURNAMENT - Sporting goods
TOURNAMENT SPECIAL - Sporting goods
TRIANGULAR - Pencil

TRIPLEX - Cider mill, oil, wringer
TROJAN - Shovel, spade, wringer
TROUT - Brush
TRUE BLUE also T. B. - Numerous items
TUNA TARPON - Fishing reel
TWENTIETH CENTURY - Razor, wringer, sewing machine
TY COBB - Baseball bat
UNIVERSE - Washboard
UTICA FIRE ARMS COMPANY - Shotgun
UTILITY - Numerous items
VAN DYKE - Enameled ware
VAQUERO - Pocket knife
VELOX - Sewing machine
VENUS - Fishing reel
VICTORIA - Lamp assortment
VICTORY - Padlock
VIDMAR - Fishing rod
VIKING - Hair clipper
VOLO - Sewing machine
VULCAN - Bicycle spokes, shovel
WALDORF - Wringer
WALL EYE - Fishing leader
WALDEN - Pocket knife
WALTON - Fishing equipment
WARRIOR - Shovel
WAUCONDA - Buggy whip
WAVELET - Boat oar
WEST END - Lawn tennis racket
WESTERN ARMS COMPANY - Gun
WEST'S - Shovel
WESTMINSTER - Inner tube, bicycle, wrench
WHALEBONE - Tool handle
WHISKER - Razor
WHITE CLAD - Refrigerator, enameled ware
WHITE CROSS - Paint
WHITE LINE - Enameled ware
WIGHTMAN'S - Bit brace, bit extension, axe stone
WILLIAMETTE - Fishing line
WILSON - Stove, kitchen range
WINDERMERE - Toilet paper
WINNER - Numerous items
WINTER'S - Recoil pad
WIRELESS - Padlock
WISCONSIN - Axe handle
WIZARD - Buggy whip
WONDER - Numerous items
WOODPECKER - Axe
WORLD'S FAIR - Padlock
WYMAN'S - Shovel
WYOMING - Axe handle
XPERT - Fishing leader
XX DOUBLE EXTRA - Washboard
YELLOW JACKET - Baseball
YELLOW STONE - Fishing equipment
YOUNG AMERICA - Gun
YUMA - Wood heater

ZULU - Paint